PRAYER AND HEALING IN ISLAM

with addendum of

25 Remedies for the Sick by Said Nursi

PRAYER AND HEALING IN ISLAM

with addendum of

25 Remedies for the Sick by Said Nursi

Salih Yücel

New Jersey

Published by Tughra Books

345 Clifton Ave., Clifton,

NJ, 07011, USA

www.tughrabooks.com

Library of Congress Cataloging-in-Publication Data Available

ISBN: 978-1-59784-242-6

Printed by
Pasifik Ofset, İstanbul - Turkey

CONTENTS

TABLES

ACKNOWLEDGEMENTS

I gratefully acknowledge the invaluable assistance of my advisor, Dr. Carole Bohn, associate professor of pastoral psychology at Boston University's School of Theology. She gave advice throughout my D.Min studies, feedback through each step of my research, and help in writing my thesis. Dr. Bohn provided excellent advice whenever I needed it, even in the summer when she was away. She guided me with professional excellence and patience.

I acknowledge Professor Merlin Swartz from the Department of Religion at Boston University, particularly for giving guidelines about incorporating the history of spiritual healing in traditional Islam. His significant feedback also helped me to complete this project.

Wayne M. Dinn, neuropsychological research scientist, graciously struggled with me editing each chapter of this thesis. His most valuable contribution was analyzing and organizing the research data using Statistical Package for the Social Sciences (SSPS). He gave his precious time generously. I thank him as both an intellectual and a long-time friend.

I thank Burak Alptekin, MD, for instructing me about vital signs and assisting with analyzing physiological data.

I extend my thanks to Partner Human Research Committee (PHRC) for allowing me to carry out this study, as well as Brigham and Women's Hospital (a teaching affiliated of Harvard Medical School) where I recruited patients and conducted this research. BWH staff attended to my research needs.

BWH patients kindly accepted participating voluntarily in this study, contributing to a greater understanding of the relationship between prayer and Muslim patients' well-being.

Finally, I would like to offer my sincere gratitude to my wife, for her patience and understanding of the life of a full-time chaplain and student. Each of my children encouraged me to complete this thesis. My special thanks to my daughter, Esma Yucel, who used her knowledge as an English major to correct grammatical errors and type this thesis.

INTRODUCTION

Praying for health is a significant Islamic custom. That is, prayer for healing is an important tradition of Prophet Muhammad, peace be upon him, (*Sunnah*) and has become a vital part of Muslim culture. Almost all Muslims, practicing and non-practicing, engage in some form of healing prayer. The practice of praying for health and recovery from illness is encouraged not only by theological reasons, but also by sociocultural and economic factors, which will be discussed later.

When discussing the power of healing prayer with Muslims, many individuals maintain that their relatives or friends have benefited from such prayer. I have rarely encountered an individual who prayed for healing and did not benefit from it, whether physically or psychologically.

In the Qur'an, Muslims are commanded to offer supplication (*du'a*) during times of trouble (i.e., both personal difficulties and widespread calamities such as physical or mental illness, war, natural disasters, and economic turmoil). The faithful is also commanded to remember God and pray in moments of joy as thanksgiving. Support for the healing power of prayer can be found in the Qur'an.

> *And your Lord says, "Call on Me; I will answer your (prayer). (40:60)*

> *And when (O Prophet) My servants ask you about Me, then surely I am near. I answer the prayer of the supplicant when he prays to Me. So let them respond to My call (without hesitation), and believe and trust in Me (in the way required of them), so that they may be guided to spiritual and intellectual excellence and right conduct. (2:186)*

> *Call upon your Lord (O humankind) with humility and in the secrecy of your hearts. Indeed your Lord does not love those who exceed the bounds. (7:55)*

Say, "My Lord would not care for you were it not for your prayer. Now that you have denied (His Message), the inescapable punishment will cleave to you." (25:77)

Various verses in the Qur'an state that true peace of mind and spiritual tranquility can be found by having faith in Allah and remembering His presence during prayer. The Qur'an declares:

Pray for the believers because that is a source of security, serenity and tranquility for them. (9:103)

Those who believe, and whose hearts find rest in the remembrance of Allah, do the hearts find rest in the remembrance of Allah. Those who believe and do right, joy and true happiness is for them and a beautiful plea of find return. (13:28-29)

In the Qur'an, there is mention of pre-Islamic prophets and their adherents offering supplication during distress and illness. Adam, the father of humankind, called upon God for forgiveness when he had committed an error that lead to his being cast out of Paradise (2:36-37).

Prophet Abraham asked God to cure his affliction, saying *"When I am ill, it is He who cures me"* (26:80). He believed that *"If God touches you with an affliction, no one can remove it but He"* (6:17). The Prophet Zakariah prayed for a child, and was blessed with a son when his wife was well past childbearing age (19:1-13).

The Prophet Yunus (Jonah) was swallowed by a large fish or whale on a stormy night. Exhausted and trapped in the belly of the sea creature, he cried out to God, saying *"There is no god other than You. Glory be onto You! Indeed, I was among the wrongdoers"* (21:17). The Prophet Isa (Jesus) held the power to heal the blind and the leper by God's will (5:109-110).

Another well-known example of supplication during times of distress and illness is Prophet Ayyub (Job) who was afflicted with numerous illnesses. He demonstrated extraordinary patience and devotion to God during his illness. When the worms generated by his wounds penetrated to his heart and his tongue, the seat of the remembrance and knowledge of God, he feared that his duty of worship would suffer, and so he said in supplication, not for the sake of his own comfort, but for the sake of his worship of God, *"O Lord! Harm has afflicted me. My remembrance of You with my tongue and my worship of You with my heart will suffer"* (21:83). God accepted Prophet Ayyub's sincere supplication and granted him good health (Nursi, 1995, 21-23).

The prophets described above serve as role models for Muslims. Prophet Muhammad, peace be upon him, followed his predecessors' actions and prayed during illnesses and offered prayers for others afflicted with various diseases. He was granted similar miracles that were bestowed upon previous prophets.

In hadith books of both Sunni and Shi'a Muslims and biographies of Prophet Muhammad, peace be upon him, there are chapters dedicated to supplication and passages related to healing prayer through medical means and miracles. These narrations form the basis of a religious science called *Tibb an-Nabawi*, Medicine of the Prophet. Foremost of compilers and writers include Ibn al-Qayyim al-Jawziyyah (d. 1351), Muhammed Ibn Ahmed Al-Dhahabi (1274–1348) and Jalal Ad-Din al-Suyuti (1445–1505). Books compiling the supplications of the Prophet, his Companions, and the saints have been produced which contain details indicating when specific supplications should be made.

Sa'd ibn Abi Waqqas was one of the ten Companions given the glad tidings of Paradise, military commander during the life of the Prophet, the commander-in-chief of the Muslim army during the reign of Caliph Umar, and the conqueror of Iran. In Qadi Iyad's (1083-1149) *Shifa ash-Sharif* (Sacred Healing), a book on Prophetic healing, Sa'd narrated:

> I was beside Allah's Prophet in the battle of Uhud... In the course of this, Qatada bin an-Nu'man [one of the Companions] was hit by an arrow, and one of his eyeballs poked out. God's Prophet, with his auspicious blessed hand, placed the eyeball back in its socket. The eye healed at once, as if nothing had happened to it, and became even better than the other one.

Reported in Bukhari (810–870) and Muslim (817–875), two authentic hadith compilations named after their compilers, it is stated that Prophet Muhammad, peace be upon him, had appointed his cousin, Ali ibn Abi Talib, as the flag-holder at the Battle of Khaybar; however, Ali had been suffering severely from a painful eye condition. The Prophet applied his healing saliva to his [Ali's] eyes, and at that moment, the pain ceased and his eyesight became much better.

Authorities on the Prophet's biography, above all, Nasa'i (819–925), another authentic hadith compiler, records a from Uthman ibn Hunayf, a Companion of the Prophet:

A blind man came to the Prophet of God and said, "Pray for my eyes to open." God's Prophet said, "Go, make ablution, and then pray two rek'ats [cycles of ritual prayer], and say, 'O God, I ask You, while turning toward You, for the sake of Prophet Muhammad, the Prophet of Mercy. I turn toward Muhammad's Lord, for your sake and through you, asking that He uncover my sight. O God, make him my intercessor.'" He departed to do what he had been told. When he came back, his eyes had already been opened.

Hadith expert Imam al-Bayhaqi (994-1066), reports that once, the Prophet's cousin, Ali, was so ill that he could not help moaning. When he was alone and praying for his cure, the Prophet came in and said, "O my Lord, heal him!" He then said to Ali, "Stand up!" nudging him with his foot. Ali was cured at once. Moreover, Ali said, "Since then I have never caught the same illness."

Imam Bayhaqi and Nasa'i reported that Prophet Muhammad, peace be upon him, healed a boy named Muhammad ibn Khatib whose arm had been scalded with boiling water. The Prophet stroked the boy's arm and applied his saliva to it.

Abu Abdurrahman al-Yamani was one of the greatest scholars of the generation that followed the age of the Companions. Indeed, Abu Abdurrahman al-Yamani had conversed with many of the Companions. He reported that "Whenever an insane person came to God's Prophet, he was cured as soon as God's Prophet put his hand on the chest of the ill person; there was no exception to this." (Nursi, 1994, p. 173)

Abu Darda', another Companion, narrates that he heard the Prophet say:

> If any of you is suffering from anything or his brother is suffering, he should say, "Our Lord is Allah, Who is in the heaven, holy is Your name, Your command reigns supreme in the heaven and the earth, as Your mercy is in the heaven, make Your mercy in the earth. Forgive us for our sins, and our errors. You are the Lord of good men. Send down mercy from Your mercy, and remedy from Your remedy on this pain so that it is healed up." (Bukhari)

The Prophet recommended the following prayer to Anas ibn Malik, another close Companion, "O Allah! The Lord of the people, the Remover of trouble! (Please) cure (this patient), for You are the Healer. None brings about healing but You, a healing that will leave behind no ailment." (Bukhari)

According to historical sources, the Companions of the Prophet and Saints offered prayer for the ill, and witnessed the recovery of those they prayed for. Muslims implicitly believe that such prayer has both physical and spiritual benefits and have continued this tradition since the time of Prophet Muhammad, peace be upon him, based on the methods he performed them.

CRITERIA FOR HEALING PRAYER

Supplication, including healing prayer, follows a set of guidelines. Said Nursi, a leading contemporary Islamic scholar, stated that there are two forms of supplication (du'a): active and passive prayer (Nursi, 1994, p. 355). When an individual takes the necessary steps to achieve a specific outcome (e.g., seeking a return to good health through medical intervention or exercise), he or she is said to be engaging in "active" prayer. When an individual seeks help from a divine power, he or she is engaging in "passive" prayer.

A supplication is deemed acceptable when the individual engages in both active and passive prayer. An individual may offer verbal prayer alone; however, it is considered to be incomplete in seeking a

return to good health since obtaining medical treatment is also obligatory in Islam (Nursi, 1994, p. 355).

Nursi (1994) stated that supplication is "a mighty mystery of worship indeed, it is like the spirit of worship" (p. 353), referring to the
Prophet's words, "Supplication is the essence of worship." Nursi (1994)
observed:

> Through supplication, the servant proclaims his own impotence
> and poverty. The apparent aims mark the times of the supplication
> and the supplicatory worship; they are not the true benefits. The
> benefits of worship look to the hereafter. If the worldly aims are
> not obtained, it may not be said, "The supplication was not
> accepted." It should rather be said, "The time for the supplication
> has still not ended" (p. 355).

The acceptance of supplication is in God's hands, not within
human power. It is the responsibility of humans to pray at the appropriate time, particularly during a time of need. Nursi states:

> There are two ways in which voluntary supplication by word is
> acceptable. It is either accepted exactly as desired or what is better
> is granted. Also, sometimes a person makes supplication for his
> own happiness in this world, and it is accepted for the hereafter. It
> may not be said, "His supplication was rejected," but that "It was
> accepted in a more beneficial form." And likewise, since Almighty
> God is All-Wise, we seek from Him and He responds to us. But
> He deals with us according to His wisdom.
>
> A sick person should not cast aspersions on the wisdom of his doc-
> tor. If he asks for honey and the expert doctor gives him quinine,
> he may not say, "The doctor did not listen to me." Rather, the doc-
> tor listened to his sighs and moans; he heard them and responded
> to them. He provided better than what was asked for (p.356).

If the doctor complied with all the wishes of the patient, the
patient would think that he knew more than the doctor and could
heal himself. Likewise, according to Islamic theology, if God granted
what was asked for in every supplication related to the worldly realm,
people would begin thinking of themselves as all-knowing godly
beings. Nursi continues:

The best, finest, sweetest, most immediate fruit and result of supplication is this, that the person who offers it knows there is someone who listens to his voice, sends a remedy for his ailment, takes pity on him, and whose hand of power reaches everything. He is not alone in this great hostel of the world; there is an All-Generous One Who looks after him and makes it friendly. Imagining himself in the presence of the One Who can bring about all his needs and repulse all his innumerable enemies, he feels a joy and relief; he casts off a load as heavy as the world, and exclaims, "All praise be to God, the Sustainer of All the Worlds!" (p.357)

Supplication relieves the feeling of suffering alone. When others make supplication for the ill person, he or she feels that others are sympathetic and considerate. When he or she prays for herself, it relieves him or her to know that, at any given time, someone will be listening. Nursi elaborates on this:

Supplication is the spirit of worship and the result of sincere belief. For one who makes supplication shows through it that there is someone who rules the whole universe; One Who knows the most insignificant things about me, can bring about my most distant aims. Who sees every circumstance of mine, and hears my voice. In which case, He hears all the voices of all beings, so that He hears my voice too. He does all these things, and so I await my smallest matters from Him too. I ask Him for them. As the saying goes, "If I had not wanted to give, I would not have given wanting" (357).

According to Islam, medical professionals, medication, and the body's immune system are the instruments that God employs to help us regain our health. Hence, it is the duty of all Muslims to seek medical assistance when ill.

Guidelines for Making Du'a (Supplication)

Du'a may be offered at any time. However, there are parameters and recommendations for offering supplication that can be classified into three categories. These guidelines are based on the Qur'an, *Sunnah* (traditions) of Prophet Muhammad, peace be upon him, and works of Islamic scholars, including Imam al-Ghazali's (1058-1111) Book of

Supplication in *Ihya Ulum ad-Din* (The Revival of Religious Science), Imam Nawawi's (1234-1278) *Riyadh as-Saliheen* (Gardens of the Righteous), Said Nursi's (1877-1960) *The Letters* and *The Flashes,* and Wahbi Zuhayli's *The Encyclopedia of Islamic Jurisprudence.*

I. Physical and spiritual preparation before making du'a

    a. To appeal to the worldly causes and factors needed to gain what is desired. For example, if one is ill, one must seek medical treatment and take necessary steps to heal.

    b. If possible, to have ablution (wudu) and ensure that clothes are clean.

    c. To have faith that the du'a will be accepted as desired in this world, or in another form in the Hereafter.

    d. To offer supplication during auspicious times, such as during times of distress, when travelling, on Fridays, during Ramadan, on holy nights (Laylatu al-Qadr), and after obligatory prayers.

    e. If possible, to offer supplication in certain places such as in the Ka'bah in Makkah, the Prophet's Mosque in Madinah, or Masjid al-Aqsa in Jerusalem.

    f. If possible, to find a quiet place where one won't be distracted.

    g. To earn a halal (lawful) livelihood and consume halal food.

II. Conditions while making du'a

    a. To begin the du'a with *Basmalah,* in the name of God, praises to God, and blessings upon the Prophet.

    b. To offer du'a sincerely and have the heart, tongue, and mind focus on it.

    c. To ask for forgiveness from God and repent from sins committed intentionally or unintentionally.

    d. To begin praying for humanity, followed by Muslims, family and friends, and finally, oneself.

    e. To follow the format of du'a in the Qur'an or in the examples of Prophets, their companions, and saints. However, one can pray in a personal format as well.

f. To ask for realistic things and that which contains no sin or harm.

g. To not expect any worldly rewards when making du'a, but to expect all results from God, especially in the Hereafter.

h. To exert oneself and ask from the bottom of the heart. If possible, to cry when asking.

i. To conclude the du'a as it was begun, with praises to God and blessings upon Prophet Muhammad, peace be upon him.

III. Etiquette after du'a

a. Believing that accepting the supplication is within God's hands, and that God knows best, even if the supplication is not accepted for this world.

b. To remain patient in expecting results. According to the Qur'an, God answers prayers, but may not accept right away, grant what was desired in the exact form, or grant what was desired in this world.

c. To be insistent in making du'a and offer it many times. Prophet Muhammad offered certain supplications daily and throughout his lifetime.

d. To not allow oneself to feel proud if the du'a is accepted in this world, assuming that God accepted the du'a due to one's noble character. On the contrary, to ask for forgiveness once the du'a is granted to prevent pride from seeping into the soul.

e. To continue believing that the du'a will be accepted in one way or another. Just as medicine will not be effective if not given during the suitable time, in the right amount, and for the right sickness, supplication also has theological conditions which make it more valid to receive what is requested.

In most research done on the effects of supplication and prayer, the guidelines measured in medical studies have not been encompassed both scientific and religious guidelines. I examined more than two hundred articles and read many books on prayer and healing, but have yet to read about a study conducted in Western countries which follows all of the above criteria, whether the test group is Muslim or non-Muslim.

One example is Benson et. al's research team who conducted one of the most scientifically rigorous investigations on the effects of prayer on illness over a ten-year period on 1,800 patients at six different hospitals in the US. The results showed that intercessory prayer for cardiac bypass patients had no positive and lasting effect. There were no set religious guidelines for the intercessory prayer, especially for the Muslims who took part in the study (Benson et al., 2006, 940).

Few studies on prayer and healing involving Muslims follow Islamic guidelines for prayer. The results of previous research on prayer and healing may not be valid from the Islamic perspective if the guidelines are not taken into consideration.

This study has taken as many guidelines as possible into consideration. This study is part of my doctoral thesis titled, "The Effects of Prayer on Muslim Patients Well-Being", which was accepted by the School of Theology at Boston University in 2007. The monogram of the thesis is available through at the University Library. However, both this introduction and cases from my personal experiences in Chapter 5 are new additions.

Another addition is *25 Remedies for the Sick* from Said Nursi's *The Gleams*, translated by Hüseyin Akarsu. Said Nursi (1877-1960) is a contemporary Turkish Islamic scholar, thinker, and revivalist. His booklet explains and elaborates on the concept of sickness and how a Muslim should view it in light of Islamic belief. I distributed it to patients and their families during my chaplaincy work in hospitals. Both patients and their families felt a great sense of relief after reading it and became inspired to be more patient towards the difficulties they experienced.

CHAPTER I

Introduction

INTRODUCTION

Religious practices such as prayer have served as alternative medical therapies since the beginning of Islam and continue to be a common practice in the Muslim world. When a Muslim is sick, he or she would not only seek medical treatment, but also spiritual care in order to get well, or to ask God to cure the sickness. In a research study in Turkey, 73% of patients reported feeling better after prayer (Dogan 1997, 52). According to one report, 80% of psychiatric patients in the Arabian Peninsula see traditional healers who offer prayer alongside natural remedies, before they seek psychiatric help (Abdullah 1998, 99). In another survey in the Arab world, 90% indicate that they would encourage others to use Qur'anic services or prayers to improve health (Adib 2004, 106).

Healing practices involve prayer to God, the use of text from the Qur'an and *sunnah*, the practices and sayings, of Prophet Muhammad, peace be upon him. Forms of *dhikr*, invocations to God, saintly prayers, and blessed *Zamzam*, holy water, from Mecca are also used. Some healers devise various other methods, such as making amulets.

These practices have roots in the Qur'an and *sunnah*. In the Qur'an, God is referred to as *As-Shafi*, the Restorer of Health (Qur'an 41:44). Prophet Muhammad, peace be upon him, stated that for every illness, God created a cure (Al-Jawziyyah 1999, 25). Verses related to healing in the Qur'an and health practices and related *hadith*, or sayings, of Prophet Muhammad, peace be upon him, have given birth to literature and research called *Tibb Nabawi*, or Prophetic Medicine. Since the eighth century, Muslim scholars and doctors have been defining and interpreting the verses and *hadiths* according to the sciences of their time. Most scholars have supported that *du'a* does have positive effects on healing.

In pre-modern times, Muslims produced more literature on prayer and healing. Abu Bakr Muhammad ibn Zakariya al-Razi (865-925), Ibn Al-Qayyim Al Jawziyyah (d.1351), and Jalal Ad-Din Al-Suyuti (1445-1505) were among the most prominent writers on religion and health. The decline of Islamic civilization led to fewer publications. In the last quarter century, however, interest in the field of alternative medicine has increased as part of the development of medicinal knowledge. This has, in turn, encouraged Muslim scholars to revisit the matter of healing in the light of spirituality.

The question of how religious healing practices benefit or detract from the well-being of humans has been an issue of concern since the rapid developments in the field of medicine in modern times. The amount of research on the religion-health connection has increased gradually in recent decades.

> The technological advances of the past century tended to change the focus of medicine from a caring, service-oriented model to a technological, cure-oriented model.... However, in the past few decades, physicians have attempted to balance their care by reclaiming medicine's more spiritual roots, recognizing that until modern times, spirituality was often linked with health-care. (Puchalski 2001, 352-357)

Larry Dossey, Herbert Benson, Jeffrey Levin, and Harold Koenig are leading figures in field of research of religion and healing. Hundreds of articles have been written for scholarly journals. Researchers at the Mayo Clinic have reviewed 350 studies of physical health and 850 studies of mental health indicate that religion plays a role in enhancing illness prevention, coping with illnesses, and recovering (Mueller et.al. 2001, 76: 1225-1235).

Such works in the West have influenced the Muslim world as well. Contemporary interpretation of the verses of the Qur'an and *hadith* of Prophet Muhammad, peace be upon him, about healing have been examined in the light of modern findings. Fazlur Rahman (1987), Adnan Al-Tharshi (1992), Tariq bin Ali Al-Habib (1995), and Shahid Athar (1996) are among those who have found that prayer has a significant role in the recovery or coping with illness of Muslim patients. The results show that Islamic prayer can lead to reduced stress and lower blood-pressure, giving patients spiritual comfort and increasing their emotional ability to deal with their illness.

In this research, the focus is on how prayer, in particular, *salat*, *du'a*, recitation of Qur'an, and *dhikr* affects Muslim patients' well-being. This study was conducted through both a survey and empirical research. This study differs from prior studies for two reasons. First, a non-religious text was used as a control, allowing for comparisons with the religious texts. Second, the vital signs, body temperature, blood pressure, and respiratory rate, of the patient were recorded before and after the sessions.

The findings of this study can help patient-care staff better understand their Muslim patients' needs. Chaplains can make use of this information when serving Muslim patients and showing respect and understanding of Islamic prayer rituals. Families of these patients may already know the patient's spiritual needs. However, this study can educate them in the connection between prayer and healing.

This study contributes to the existing prayer and healing studies and publications in three particular ways. First, vital signs are recorded and analyzed before and after religious (i.e. prayers) and non-religious readings. Second, it will add to the current literature empirical evidence on the effects of prayer on Muslim patients. Third, the study presents consequences for misunderstanding, misinterpreting, and improperly practicing Islamic prayer.

STATEMENT OF THE PROBLEM

This study investigates how Islamic prayer (i.e., *du'a*, *dhikr*, and recitation of Qur'an) affects different aspects of patients' well-being. This research determines whether prayer contributes to or detracts from patients' well-being. The present study addresses the following issue: how does the patient respond, spiritually and physically, to prayer? The physical and spiritual condition of the patient before and after prayer will be monitored. The principal research objective of the present study is to determine whether prayer has a positive impact on physical and/or spiritual health.

HYPOTHESIS

The present study will test the following hypothesis: prayer will have positive effects on Muslim patients' well-being if it is performed according to certain criteria as set forth by Islamic texts and their interpretations by Muslim scholars.

This hypothesis is supported by traditional and contemporary scholars, both of which rely on Qur'anic verses and *Tibb Nabawi*, Prophetic medicine. Based on interpretations of these religious texts, numerous scholars maintain that prayer has physical, psychological, emotional, and spiritual benefits. Among these scholars is Abu Bakr Muhammad ibn Zakariya al-Razi, Ibn Al-Qayyim Al-Jawziyyah, Al-Suyuti, Abu Hamed Muhammad ibn Muhammad Al-Ghazali. Said Nursi, Elmalılı Hamdi Yazır, Sayyid Qutub, Adnan al-Tharshi and Tariq bin Ali Habib.

LIMITATIONS

The principal limitation of this study involves issues regarding the sample population in research. First, the sample consists of only sixty adult Muslim patients. It was impossible to recruit a patient from each Muslim country; therefore, not all Islamic sects were represented or represented equally. Nevertheless, the principal investigator tried to be as pluralistic as possible. In terms of gender and ethnic background, the principal investigator could not get equal numbers because the sample depends on general hospital distribution.

Second, the study measures are limited to short-term effects. Patients were surveyed in a period of 2-5 days.

Third, the hospital setting is not always ideal for a concentrated prayer. There are distractions such as noises from other patients, staff, and equipment.

Fourth, some answers received for the questions in the questionnaire will not be unbiased. Respondents' answers are drawn from their experiences and are dependent on their current physical, psychological, and emotional conditions. It is questionable as to how much each respondent knows the performing guidelines of prayer. This may affect their measure of the accuracy of their empirical experience and performance. However, to overcome this limitation, the principal investigator relied on interwriter reliability. Imam Talal Eid, ThD, reviewed the responses independently.

Fifth, being not fully aware of all the patient's cultural backgrounds and traditions can limit the evaluation of the answers. Before the principal investigator conducted the survey, he sought knowledge from other sources regarding the patient's cultural background by reading about their culture and asking interpreters to explain cultural norms at hospitals.

Sixth, some patients are not native English speakers or may not completely understand the terms used but the principal investigator addressed this issue through the use of interpreters.

Finally, some Muslim patients may overstate their religiosity or spirituality. This observation is based on my professional experiences as a hospital chaplain for 20 years.

The definition of prayer

Prayer may have different connotations and methods of performance. Because prayer has varying meanings in different religions, it is necessary to define for readers the meaning of prayer (i.e., a general definition and specific Islamic traditions).

The word «prayer» is derived from the Latin root *precare*, meaning "to ask for something" or "to beg." Webster's dictionary defines prayer as "entering into communion with God."

Prayer is an act of communication by humans with the sacred or holy-God, the gods, the transcendent realm, or supernatural powers.

Found in all religions in all times, prayer may be a communal or personal act utilizing various forms and techniques.

Scholars define prayer in various ways. William James (1842-1910) defines prayer as "every kind of inward communion or conversation with the power recognized as divine." (James 1963, 5). Jean Daujat states that the Latin word for "to pray" is *orare*, which derives from the word for mouth, and it means not "to ask", but "to speak." Prayer is an address directed to God or to a superior power in which we reveal our needs and implore that they be fulfilled (1964, 8).

Karl Rahner, (1904-1984) an influential German theologian, describes prayer as adoration, thanksgiving, oblation, penitence, intercession, praise and petition, and views prayer as a response to God's call and a free act by a man or woman. Prayer has been defined as "any personal, impersonal or transpersonal way to express communion with the sacred" (Delong 1998, 65-66).

From another point of view, "Prayer is the raising of one's mind and heart to God or the requesting of good things from God" (Ruland 1994, 13). This definition includes aspects of both emotion and cognition in the petition to God.

Dossey defines prayer as "communication with the Absolute" (1998, 10). This definition is more general due to the range of options of communication with God, such as silent prayer from the heart, verbal prayer, or congregational prayers. This means that prayer does not need to be verbal only; even silence, contemplation, or meditation can be a form of talking to God.

Prayer in Islam

Ritual prayer, known as *salat*, is one of the pillars of Islam. However, *salat* is different than the personal prayer or invocation associated with the Christian faith. In Islam, that is called the *du'a*, or supplication, formal and informal. Formal *du'as* are found in the Qur'an, *hadith*, and religious texts. Informal *du'as* are personally structured or spontaneous.

In the Qu'ran, the word *salat* can be applied to God, angels, and humans (33:56). For God, it means that He inclines towards being merciful to humans; for angels, it means that they ask forgiveness for humans; for humans, it means supplicating to God (Al-Ghazali 2004, 4).

In Islamic texts, prayer is referred to as *salat* and *du'a*. Muslim scholars have observed that *salat*, a form of ritual prayer, has positive effects on the sick. *Salat* is a religious process involving specific movements and invocations. It begins with the takbir, raising hands to face level. A person stands straight, a position called the *qiyam*, and recites Qur'anic verses. He or she then bows with hands on the knees in the *ruku* position. After standing up straight again, he or she goes down to prostrate, *sujuud*. After two *sujuuds*, a person is in *juluus*, a sitting position, and finally, ends with the *salam*, turning head to right then left shoulder. Each movement and position is accompanied by certain praises to God, such as *Allahu akbar*, "God is great". It is about professing gratitude and glorifying and exalting God (Al-Ghazali 2004, 4).

The word *du'a* comes from the roots of d-a-wa in Arabic. This word literally means "to call upon, to lead someone to something, to invite someone, or to grieve after a deceased person" (Soysaldi 1996, 13).

The word *du'a* is defined in several ways in the Qur'an: as a form of worship (10:106), a means of asking for aid (2:23), God's call to humans (17:52), and praise to God (17:101). The characteristic common to all four definitions is *du'a* as a form of communication between a person and God.

The technical meaning of *du'a* has been defined by Prophet Muhammad, peace be upon him, as "the essence of worship" and "the essence of servitude" (Canan 1993, 487).

Some Muslim scholars define *du'a* as follows. Said Nursi (1887-1960) suggested that there are three types of *du'as*: first, the request with one's condition, such as acting through causes to get the desired effect. If a student wishes to pass an exam, his or her act of studying leads to passing, thus making the act of studying an active form of *du'a*. The second type is to desire from the heart, and the third is the direct verbal request arising from desperate need at that time (Nursi

1994, 353-354). *Du'a* is a symbol of servitude from the servant to God, and a mark of God's mercy to his servant (Canan 1993, 487). Another definition is to ask God earnestly from the heart in silence (488).

Although the precise definitions of *du'a* vary from scholar to scholar, it is generally viewed as a form of communication between a person and a higher power. Traditional Muslim scholars view *du'a* as a form of worship and an asking from God. Contemporary Qur'anic commentator and a Turkish Muslim theologian Hamdi Yazır (1877-1942) defined *du'a* as "the subject to appeal for in a manner that indicates his need to God by thanking and glorifying Him" (1992, 2194). Muhammad Ikbal (1873-1938), a Pakistani theologian, philosopher, and poet, viewed *du'a* as a form of deep feeling of humankind towards the Creator for their needs (Dogan 1997, 7). Nursi stated that *du'a* is "mighty mystery of worship; indeed, it is like the spirit of worship;" to ask God for that which they cannot grasp with their own power and will (1994, 353-354). Gülen states that *du'a* is asking God for something which the human cannot attain by his or her power (Dogan 1997, 15). Cilaci stated that the *du'a* flows "from the younger to the older, from the bottom to the top, from an inferior to a superior" (1965, 528). The first part of the definition applies to human-human relations and not human-God relations. Kayiklik views *du'a* as removing the obstacles between oneself and God, allowing them to reunite (1994, 23-24).

Sufis see *du'a* as mystical love of God, an act of a lover asking something from the beloved (Seriati 1993, 51). According to Sufi scholars, *du'a* is the manifestation of God's love to humans (44). Abd al-Karim Hawazin Al-Qushayri (d.1072), one of the great mystic leaders who established the principles of Sufism, stated "Only the tongue of beginners speaks prayers. The prayer of Gnostic consists in deeds that of the perfect of mystical states" (Al-Qushayri 1990, 11). For Al-Qushayri, individual verbal prayers constitute of the first levels of spirituality. This means that as the person advances spiritually, his or her form of prayer will be the actions instead of the verbal supplication, like the aforementioned example of the student. Another definition by Sufis is that prayer is not petitioning or asking; it is, in essence, everlasting praise (Schimmel 1952, 112-125).

In light of the aforementioned definitions, *du'a* falls into either one of two categories: communication or supplication. Communication is when one calls upon or invites. This can further be divided into two subcategories. A person can ask from God either through silence or praying from the heart or action. Supplication is when *du'a* is in form of a verbal request.

SIGNIFICANCE OF THE STUDY

This study is significant in that it utilizes and extends an emerging research methodology in religious studies from an Islamic viewpoint. This methodology measures the effects of prayer by interviewing patients and monitoring patients' vital signs, then analyzing the data to find out whether there is a relationship between health and prayer.

This research traces its roots to the Qur'an, *Tibb Nabawi* (Prophetic medicine, i.e. the techniques and medicine that were applied and recommended by Prophet Muhammad, peace be upon him, contemporary research, and the perspectives of well-known Muslim scholars. However, more research studies about the application of *Tibb Nabawi* to the context of modern medicine are needed. Such a study has not been conducted from an Islamic viewpoint, but there have been studies on the effect of prayer on members of other faiths by Dossey (1993), Chan (1994), Benson (1995), Stavros (1997), and others.

The research not only relies on theological, psychological and medical studies and sources, but also on my extensive experience dealing with patients in hospitals. In my professional experiences, the principal investigator has observed most patients and their families benefiting from prayer. Their morale increased, stress was reduced, and their coping process was better.

This thesis will contribute to an understanding of how prayer can be exercised with the healing practice. Second, the study can guide pastoral caregivers and healers working with Muslim patients, and, hopefully, enhance their effectiveness. Third, it will also present different techniques of approaching and comforting the patient for pastoral caregivers as well as medical staff. Fourth, the result of this study may encourage the Muslim community to educate more clergy for providing chaplaincy services in health institutions. Fifth, the research will stress the significance of prayer and the importance of performance in accordance to Islamic guidelines in order to avoid negative consequences. Sixth, this is the first study of its kind in the US. Prior studies have been conducted in Muslim countries (nations where Islam is the primary religion). Finally, if the hypothesis is supported by the findings, then Muslim patients can further understand the benefits of prayer if prayer is practiced properly.

CHAPTER II

Literature Review

LITERATURE REVIEW

INTRODUCTION

I n this chapter, the principal investigator reviewed the literature and established a theoretical foundation for this study. First, the principal investigator described the contributions of early interpreters of Islamic texts and pioneers in the field of prayer and healing. This includes the views of traditional scholars, *hakeem*, or physician-scholars, and philosophers from the golden age of Islamic civilization as well as contemporary researchers. The principal investigator has divided the review into two subsections: 1) theological considerations; and 2) theoretical considerations.

THEOLOGICAL CONSIDERATIONS

Healing in the Qur'an

In order to understand the concept of prayer and healing in Islam, it is necessary to look to the definitions of healing found in the Qur'an and its exegesis, and the *sunnah* of Prophet Muhammad, peace be upon him, along with scholarly interpretations. It is a principle of Islamic faith to believe and accept the Qur'an as the word of God and follow the *sunnah*. As a result, Muslims have continued to employ the healing practices of Prophet Muhammad, peace be upon him, described in the *hadith* collections. However, the central aim of the Qur'an is to influence and provide guidance for human conduct (Rahman 1987, 11). It is, of course, not a scientific or medical text, but it is considered to be a "restorer of health" (41:44) which has been taken by Muslims to mean that its guidance leads to spiritual, psychological, and physical health (Rahman 1987, 21). In Muslim society, individuals will commonly employ conventional medical treatment as well as spiritual remedies.

Healing in Islam has been described in the Qur'an and *sunnah* (the tradition of Prophet Muhammad, peace be upon him) and involves both physical and spiritual factors. Verses and *hadith* relating to both components are explained in the *hadith* and scholarly texts. Two verses in the Qur'an (9:14, 26:80) refer to God as *As-Shafi*, "The Healer." The word *shifa*, healing, occurs in different grammatical forms in six verses in the Qur'an.

In the following sections, the principal investigator briefly described the perspectives of at-Tabari (828-923) and Ibn Kathir (1301-1373), two highly influential Qur'anic commentators, along with those of Al-Razi (865-925), Qutb, and Yazır.

1. *And (Allah) shall heal the breast of the believers* (9:14).

At-Tabari, a notable Qur'anic scholar, viewed this *shifa* as a remedy for spiritual diseases of the heart (1995, 117). Ibn Kathir defines the word *shifa* in a similar manner (1995, 169).

2. *Mankind there has come to you as a guidance from your lord and a healing from the (diseases) in your hearts and for those who believe, a guidance and mercy* (10:57).

Ibn Kathir explains that the healing described in this verse should be interpreted as indicating that the Qur'an heals doubts of the heart (1995, 456). At-Tabari defines the healing described in this verse as a way to heal spiritual diseases of the heart, such as greed, haughtiness, selfishness (1995, 160).

3. *And we sent down in the Qur'an such things that have healing and mercy for the believers* (15:82).

Al-Razi also suggested that healing involves both physical and spiritual processes (Canan 1993, 78). According to at-Tabari and Ibn Kathir, the Qur'an heals hypocrisy, doubts, and spiritual diseases of the heart (79). Nursi stated that the Qur'an is a healing force for those who believe in and practice its message (2005, 153).

4. *There issues from within the bodies of the bee a drink of varying colors wherein is healing for mankind* (16:69).

The drink mentioned in this verse is honey, making healing, in this context, physical, according to Qur'anic scholars, who parallel this verse with a related *hadith*.

5. *And when I am ill, it is (Allah) who cures me* (26:80).

In their commentary on this verse, At-Tabari (105) and Ibn Kathir interpret this as indicating a physical healing of the body (1995, 6-170).

6. *And declare (O Muhammad) that (the Qur'an) is guidance and healing for the believers* (41:44).

As in second verse (10:57), the Qur'an is the healer of spiritual diseases such as haughtiness, hypocrisy, and vanity (at-Tabari 1995, 159).

Qutb defines healing in these verses as spiritual healing (3:1799, 5:2602, 3127) except the verse 16:69, wherein the verse describing the healing powers of honey refers to a physical process (1976). It is said that the Qur'an can remove doubts, greed, temptation, and hopelessness from the hearts of the believers. It can give believers security, confidence, and patience in the face of adversities and illnesses (Qutb 1976).

Nursi stated that all forms of healing are manifestations of *As-Shafi*, The Healer, a name of God. This name will reflect on any person or creature that resorts to proper healing methods. Nursi did not make any distinction between religious and secular sciences. He viewed all sciences as manifestations of God (Nursi 2005, 351-355).

Two more verses in the Qur'an relate to health indirectly:

> ... *(A)nd make not your own hands contribute to (your) destruction; but do good; for Allah loves those who do good.* (2:195)

> ...*Nor kill (or destroy) yourselves: for verily Allah has been to you Most Merciful!* (4:29)

According to Qur'anic commentators, these verses ask the believer to take precaution against all diseases (spiritual, physical, or psychological) and not let the lack of preventative measures cause self-destruction. Spiritual precautions can include prayer in the face of stress, anxiety, and depression (Rahman1987, 125).

Throughout Islamic history, scholars have commented on which chapter or verse in the Qur'an and *du'as* can be used for physical, spiritual, or emotional healing (Canan 1993, 76). Prophet Muhammad, peace be upon him, had already mentioned some of these chapters or verses, but commentators have expanded on these verses based on their knowledge and experiences. These books are referred to as *Khavass al-Qur'an* (Miraculous Properties of the Qur'an). The earliest of these belongs to ninth-century writer al- Hakim al-Tamimi. In this work, the "miraculous properties" including their curative properties for various diseases and mental illnesses, of virtually each passage of the Qur'an are discussed (Rahman 1987, 89) and include remedies for various diseases and mental illnesses.

The Islamic tradition of healing with prayer dates back to Prophet Muhammad, peace be upon him. Due to the presence of verses relating to healing in the Qur'an and the *hadiths* (sayings of Muhammad, peace be upon him), the science of Islamic healing has received much attention. The Qur'anic verses regarding healing have been interpreted literally and in the context of Muhammad's prophethood, which lasted about 23 years. The Qur'an was revealed in allotments over that period. The verses are directly related to the events, circumstances and needs of the period of Muhammad's prophethood.

In light of the Qur'anic verses and *hadiths*, books have been and are still being written on *Tibb Nabawi*, Prophetic Medicine. *Hadiths* about healing have been grouped into a separate section in *hadith* collections. There are many collections of the traditional sayings of Prophet Muhammed, peace be upon him, on the subject of medicine and healing by religious scholars and physicians. The following scholars are well known and their interpretations are often quoted by other scholars: Abu Bakr al-Razi (865-925), Shams-ul- Din al Dhahabi (1274-1348), Abu Abdullah Mohamed Ibn al-Qayyim al-Jawziyyah (d.1351) and Jalal-ul-Din Abd-ul -Rahman ibn Abi Bakr Al-Suyuti (1445- 1505) (Al-Suyuti 1962, 41). There are many *hakeem*, physicians and men of wisdom, who wrote about healing and medicine in Islam such as Abu Yusuf Ya'qub ibn Ishak al-Kindi (d.873), and Ibn Sina, or Avicenna (d.1037). Contemporary scholars include Elmalılı Hamdi Yazır, Said Nursi, and Sayyid Qutb.

Scholars who view the Qur'an as the source of healing rely on the verses on shifa and an incident in the Prophet's life, narrated Abu Said Al-Khudri:

> Some of the companions of the Prophet came across a tribe amongst the tribes of the Arabs, and that tribe did not entertain them. While they were in that state, the chief of that tribe was bitten by a snake (or stung by a scorpion). They said, (to the companions of the Prophet), "Have you got any medicine with you or anybody who can treat with *Ruqya*?" The Prophet's companions said, "You refuse to entertain us, so we will not treat (your chief) unless you pay us for it." So they agreed to pay them a flock of sheep. One of them (the Prophet's companions) started reciting Surat-al-Fatiha (Chapter of Opening) and gathering his saliva and spitting it (at the snake-bite). The patient got cured and his people presented the sheep to them, but they said, "We will not take it unless we ask the Prophet (whether it is lawful)." When they asked him, he smiled and said, "How do you know that Surat-al-Fatiha is a *ruqya*? Take it (flock of sheep) and assign a share for me (Bukhari).

In this hadith, *ruqya* means a charm, spell, or incantation. It has been used as a means of seeking a cure for any illness by reciting Qur'an and making *du'a* to God.

The Prophet taught that healing should be conducted only in accordance with Qur'anic teachings. In addition, Prophet Muhammad, peace be upon him, made supplications for the ill, including the mentally and spiritually ill. However, some scholars of Islam, such as Ibn Khaldun (1332-1406), maintained that the Prophet had been sent to teach only sacred law and not medicine. Such an interpretation is based on the following discourse between Muhammad, peace be upon him, and his companions. Muhammad, peace be upon him, had advised his companions to artificially fertilize palm-trees. Later, some of the companions informed Muhammad, peace be upon him, that his advice led to a bad crop, to which the Prophet replied, "You know better than I matters pertaining to this world" (Rahman 1987, 33). Rahman and other Muslim scholars used this hadith to emphasize the Prophet's role as a messenger rather than a healer. Omar Kasule, deputy dean of the Faculty of Medicine at International Islamic University in Malaysia, states that *Tibb Nabawi* (Prophetic medicine) did not cover every conceivable disease at the time of the Prophet nor can it cover all illnesses today or in the future in various parts of the world. He supports Ibn Khaldun's view and states that hadith should not be viewed as the textbook of medicine, but should only be used for the diseases they dealt with (Barnes & Sered 2005, 410).

Healing the chief of the tribe by reciting the Chapter of *Al-Fatiha* (The Opening) might be a divine blessing, called *karama* in Islamic terminology. However, this particular action in the above *hadith* cannot be applied as a universal cure for every scorpion sting. Yet, a person who has been stung by a scorpion must seek both medical treatment and can recite from the Chapter of *Al-Fatiha*. This will be appropriate in regards to all the verses and *hadiths* related to healing.

Based on this comparison, it is incorrect to seek treatment only with the Qur'an or hadith. Furthermore, it is an established practice of Islamic interpretation to examine the context of the selected text. Some texts were directed to certain people or refer to specific occasions or events. Not researching the context can lead to much misunderstanding. If a Muslim understood this event literally, he or she would apply the same method if he or she was stung and not apply to modern medicine. Due to such misunderstanding or ignorance, some Muslims do not seek medical treatment.

The *sunnah* of Prophet Muhammad, peace be upon him, is the first source for Qur'anic exegesis and the second source of Islam. It is necessary to review the relationship between prayer and healing in the *sunnah*.

Healing in the sunnah

Muslim scholars view the *sunnah* as the second source of religion, while the Qur'an is the primary source. Following the *sunnah* is ordered in the Qur'an (59:7, 4:80, 3:31, 33:21) as Prophet Muhammad, peace be upon him, is the ultimate role model for Muslims. The number of Prophetic sayings, or *hadith*, in the area of medicine, prayer, and health led to the development of an entire discipline known as *Tibb Nabawi* (Prophetic medicine). These *hadith* include both cures and preventative measures (Barnes & Sered 2005, 409). Imam Bukhari, the primary sources of Prophetic sayings, narrated 129 *hadiths* directly related to medicine, prayer, and healing, and has compiled two books on physical and spiritual healing (Al-Suyuti 1962, 130-141). Other *hadith* collections also have chapters dedicated to healing.

Healing *hadith* can be divided into three categories. First, there are *hadiths* that encourage medical treatment and seek to give broad principles of health. Second are *hadiths* that are comprised of putative statements of Prophet Muhammad, peace be upon him, on particular diseases and health problems as well as techniques used to treat them, both medical and spiritual. The third is the role of these *hadiths* in the literature of the Prophetic medicine (Rahman, 1987, 34).

The Prophet used three types of remedies for various ailments: natural, divine, and or a combination of both natural and divine cures (Al-Jawziyyah 1999, 35). The spiritual techniques utilize the patient's energy and the power contained in the devotions and supplications as well as the meditations of Prophet Muhammad, peace be upon him, and saints. The focus of this section is on the *hadiths* related to both prayer and healing.

Listed below are some of the prominent *hadiths* about prayer and healing:

> Every illness has a cure, and when the proper cure is applied, it ends Allah's willing (Al-Jawziyyah 1999, 24).

> Prophet Muhammad, peace be upon him, said, "Treatment is a part of destiny" (Canan 1993, 132).

When the Prophet heard that people in a certain village contracted a contagious disease, he ordered that the villagers stay in the village and outsiders stay outside, thus quarantining the sickness. The Prophet made seeking treatment obligatory on ill persons (Al-Jawziyyah 1999, 25).

Usame bin Shuraik narrated that "I was with the Prophet when the Bedouins came to him and said 'O Messenger of Allah should we seek medicine?' He said, 'Yes, O slave of Allah, seek medicine, for Allah has not created a disease except that he has also created it cure, except for one illness.' They said "What was that?' He said 'Old age' (Al-Jawziyyah 1999, 25).

Allah has not sent down a disease except that He has also sent down its cure; Whoever knows it (the cure), knows it, and whoever is unaware of it (the cure), he is unaware of it (the medicine) while those who are ignorant of it are unaware of it (Nasai, Ibn Majah).

Make use of two cures: honey and the Qur'an (Ibn Majah).

A man came to the Prophet and said: O Messenger of God, you have forbidden the recitation of verses over the sick. Yet I can cure scorpion bites by these recitations. The Prophet replied: He who among you is able to help his brother, let him do so (Al-Suyuti 1962, 131).

Ali narrated that the Prophet said: The Qur'an is the best of all medicines (Ibn Maja, Al-Suyuti 1962, 131).

Abu Huraira said: The Prophet saw me when I was asleep and I was writhing with my pain in the stomach. He said, "Does your stomach give you pain?" And I answered, "Yes, O Prophet." Then he said, "Arise and pray; for verily in prayer there is cure" (Ibn Maja, Al-Suyuti 1962, 157).

Said Uthman ibn abi al- As: A man complained to the Prophet of a pain that he felt in his body ever since he had become Muslim. The Prophet replied to him: Put your right hand on place of the pain and seven times: I fly to the protection of God and His power from the evil which I find (Al-Suyuti 1962, 159).

Khalid bin al-Walid said: O Prophet, I cannot sleep at night by reason of my insomnia. So the Prophet replied: When you go to your bed to sleep then say: O God, Lord of Seven Heavens and whatsoever is upon them and Lord of Devils and of those they have mislead, be for me a Helper against all the evils of creation if any of them oppresses me. May Your help stay long with me. Exalted be Your praise. There is no God other than You and no God excepting You (Al-Suyuti 1962, 159).

A man should indeed pray God for good health. But if God bestows sickness, it should be receive with patience, with resignation and with thankfulness (Al-Suyuti 1962, 162).

The Prophet said to Umar: If you go into the room of a sick man, beg him to pray to God for you. For the prayer of a sick person is like to the prayer of angels (162).

It was habit of the Prophet whenever he visited the sick or if a sick man was brought to him, to say: O Thou God of people, derive away all harm and cure the cure which leaves no sickness, which leaves behind no trace of diseases. Then the sick man should read to himself the opening chapter of the Qur'an (163).

Al-Tirmidhi extracted from Abu Harira the following tradition. The Folio 29 Prophet, whenever anything worried him, would raise his head to Heaven and say: Glory be to God, the Great. And about 'Abd-Ullah ibn Mas'ud there is the following tradition. He used to say: No worshipper who is afflicted with care & grief and who says: O God, I am your worshipper with a father & mother who worshipped you. Every thing of mine is in your hands. Precise is your Wisdom and just are your Decrees. I beg of you by every name by which you style yourself or that you have sent down into the Holy Book or that you have told to any one of your Creation or that you have preferred to keep unknown within your self, I beg of you that you make the Quran the spring of my heart, the light of my breast, the banisher of my grief, and the remover of my care. From no one who says this will God fail to drive away grief and care and set up joy in their stead. This is related by Ahmed in his al-Masnid and Ibn Habban in his al-Sahih (64).

What do you think about the very words of God and the reported saying of 'All: The Quran is the best of all medicines. Bin Maja reports this saying (131).

From 'Abd-Ullah bin 'Umr comes the following tradition: If any one of you suffer from sleeplessness, let him say: I take refuge in

> all the words of God from His anger, from punishment, from the
> evil of His worshippers, and from the instigations of the devils,
> should they come. Surely these words will not fail you (157).

> O Bilal, let us take rest in prayer. And again when he said: I have
> made my comfort in prayer because from it man derives pleasure
> and the pleasure of it brings comfort and because prayer contains
> the excellencies of this world and of the next (158-159).

Muslims have practiced spiritual healing alongside physical healing due to the Prophet's practices. However, because the *hadiths* are not a comprehensive book of medicine, only some illnesses and methods of treatment in his time are covered. Therefore, it is important to understand these practices in their context. For this reason, many Muslim physicians, scholars, and *hakeem* have explored and written about the Prophetic healing practices in detail. As mentioned in the Healing in the Qur'an section, traditional scholars of hadith and Muslims physician-philosophers include Ibn Al-Qayyim Al-Jawziyyah, Al Dhahabi, Al-Ghazali, Ibn Sina (also known as Avicenna), and Al-Suyuti, while contemporary scholars and Muslim physicians include Said Nursi, Sayyid Kutub, Adnan At-Tahrshi, Tariq bin Ali Al-Habib, Ridwan Faqeeh, and Shahid Athar. Their theories are reviewed in the next section.

THEORETICAL CONSIDERATIONS

I will discuss the theoretical literature regarding prayer and healing in two sections: first, through Islamic sources, and second, through Western sources. Islamic sources include historical and current research as my primary research is about Islamic prayer and healing. The discussion of Western sources includes only current empirical studies as secondary evidence.

Islamic sources

The relationship between prayer and healing has been discussed in the Islamic literature since the ninth century (Rahman 1987, 48). This discussion began with the collection of *hadiths* (Prophetic sayings) on the subject of medicine and healing, and was later followed by works on *Tibb Nabawi* (Prophetic medicine). Three works are prominent and extensively quoted by other scholars. These were written by Abu Bakr Al-Razi (865-925), Shams-ul- Din al Dhahabi (1274-1348), and Ibn Al-Qayyim al-Jawziyyah (d.1351) (Al-Suyuti, 1962, p.41). Later scholars, such as Jalal-ul-Din al-Suyuti (1445-1505), based their works on the three aforementioned texts.

Early Muslim scholars did not distinguish between secular medicine and *Sharia* law Imam As-Shafi (d. 819), founder of the Shafi Islamic school of thought, or *fiqh*, religious jurisprudence, posited that medicine is one third of human knowledge and Muslims should acquire an understanding of medical science (Rahman 1987, 48). Al-Dhahabi stated that all Muslims agree that it is meritorious to seek healing when one is sick because of the Prophet's comment "get medical treatment," making such treatment obligatory (Al-Dhahabi 1996, 103-104). Imam al-Ghazali viewed the study of both medicine and religion-based healing practices as obligatory (Rahman 1987, 38). This clearly establishes that medicine is a religious service (Rahman 1987, 39). Abu Bakr Al-Razi stated that students must pursue medical studies after mastering the Sacred Law, which includes *Sharia* and Islamic ethics (Rahman 1987, 39). This worldview led scholars to pursue both Islamic legal training and medical studies, and religious scholars functioned as both doctors and jurists. It is interesting to note that the term for physician is *hakim*, meaning wise man or philosopher. The term clearly reflected the aforementioned worldview, and such people were regarded as natural leaders, charismatic people who are influential (Dols 1984, 37). They attempted to spiritualize medicine and to set a high religious value on the practice of medicine. Moreover, they were motivated by a desire to focus the attention of Muslims on medicine (Rahman 1987, 42). These physicians applied both physical and spiritual treatments, such as prayer, Qur'anic recitation, and spiritual music, to their patients. Medicine was part of the curriculum of *madrasas* where religion and secular sciences were generally taught for a great period of Islamic history.

Towards the nineteenth century, less emphasis was placed on medical knowledge due to the influence of positivism, specialization of medicinal sciences, absence of large hospitals, and decay of Muslim civilization (Rahman 1987, 75).

Muslim scholars on healing

Muslim scholars maintained that healing involved physical, psychological, and spiritual processes. In order to overcome illness, a person must apply both physical treatment and spiritual strengthening.

The different forms of worship in Islam (*salat*, *du'a*, recitation of Qur'an, *dhikr*) develop a mentality which leads to spiritual healing and well-being, along with physical healing and the alleviation of physical suffering (i.e., overcoming illness).

Al-Razi, "undoubtedly the greatest physician of the Islamic world," states that the Creator bestowed reason on man so that people can achieve contentment in this world and happiness in the Hereafter (Al-Razi 1950, 20). By applying reason, a person can reduce grief caused by illnesses or other hardships and can take certain stipulations. One of the precautions prescribed by Islam is contemplating about death and the afterlife and praying for protection from hardships, thereby training the soul to bear grief and difficulties more effectively. If an ill Muslim knows the purpose of life and believes in the existence of an afterlife, then the pains encountered during his or her earthly existence would seem insignificant compared to the greater joys awaiting him or her in the next world. The purpose of our earthly existence is to worship God (51:56-58) and attain Paradise through a life of virtue. Therefore, suffering in this transient life can be tolerated because an eternal life will follow. Some Muslims misunderstand this as a reason not to seek treatment. However, seeking treatment is an obligation as mentioned in the Theological Considerations section.

Second, after misfortunes such as illnesses and calamities have occurred, it is important to reduce or repel negative feelings like sorrow, anguish, and grief completely or to the greatest possible extent (70).

Ibn Sina supported the view of the benefits of prayer; however, he maintained that the faithful must seek proper medical treatment as well as seeking spiritual remedies (Dogan 1997, 7). In this sense, making *du'a* without seeking medical treatment does not validate the *du'a*. It is obligatory for Muslims to seek medical treatment (Rahman 1987, 48). *Du'a* is a strong recommendation by Prophet Muhammad, peace be upon him. If a Muslim makes *du'a* without seeking or intending to seek medical treatment, he or she is practicing dualism, attending to the spiritual dimension of his or her being but not the physical dimension.

Ibn Sina also recognized the value of overcoming fears and using willpower in the healing process:

> Ibn Sina states that there are physically sick people who get well through sheer willpower, and conversely, there are healthy persons who become obsessed with the idea that they are sick, so that they really become physically sick. From this he concludes that the mind, which belongs to the realm of higher metaphysical principles, "exercises lordship over matter." He illustrates this by saying that is a plank of wood is put across a street and someone is asked to walked on it, he will be able to do so quite easily. But if the same plank of wood is places across a gorge, the same person will probably be able to walk on it and may well fall if he tries. (Rahman 1987, 36)

In Islam, when a Muslim performs prayer, he or she relies on a higher and powerful being, Allah. Muslims believe that Allah is the *As-Shafi*, The Healer, and will ease the pain of the patient (if that is what is best for him or her). This decreases the patient's worry and fear of his or her illness and related problems. Anxiety reduction increases psychological comfort and enhances coping skills.

Al-Dhahabi, an influential *hakim* and a traditional Islamic scholar and historian, purports the benefits of Islamic ritual prayers are four-fold: 1) spiritual; 2) psychological; 3) physical; and 4) moral. He gave three reasons for this. First, ritual prayer is a form of worship commanded by God. Second, prayer has a psychological benefit. Concentrating on prayers diverts the mind from pain. In the physical sense, prayer allows for full bodily movements which cause some organs such

as the muscles to relax. Al-Dhahabi also asserted that prayers often pro-
duce happiness and satisfaction; they suppress anxiety and extinguish
anger (Al- Dhahabi 1996, 140; Rahman 1987, 44).

Al-Jawziyyah supported this view. He supported the common
idea among Muslims that the strong spirit of an ill person will assist
the body in overcoming illness (Rahman 1987, 42). He relies on the
following *hadith*, "Saying good words to a patient for the sake of
God, although it does not prevent any harm, still brings relief to the
patient's heart" (Canan 1993). Good words can include prayer, words
of hope, good news, or advice and will relieve the anxiety of the sick
person and bring relief to his or her heart. It can add strength to the
spirit of the sick person, further encouraging the body to fight disease
(Al-Jawziyyah 1999, 109).

Al-Jawziyyah recommended quoting from the Qur'an and *hadiths*
to psychologically prepare the sick person for the worst:

> *...give glad tidings to the patient...* (2:155).

> *And seek help in patience and the prayer* (2:45).

> *...But it is possible that you dislike a thing which is good for you* (2:116).

> *So verily, with every difficulty, there is relief. Verily, with every difficul-
> ty, there is relief* (94:5-6).

> Abu Yahya Suhaib bin Sinan (may Allah be pleased with him)
> reported that: The Messenger of Allah said, "How wonderful is
> the case of a believer; there is good for him in everything and this
> applies only to a believer. If prosperity attends him, he expresses
> gratitude to Allah and that is good for him; and if adversity befalls
> him, he endures it patiently and that is better for him" (Muslim).

In these and other related verses and *hadiths*, there is a psychological and spiritual comfort for two reasons. First, the slave of Allah,
his family and wealth are Allah's exclusive property that Allah has
loaned to the slave. When Allah takes back some of what he has
loaned the slave, He is the Owner who takes back what belongs to
Him. (Al-Jawziyyah 1999, 170-171). The term slave in Islamic texts

is similar in meaning to the word "subject." Second, "the anguish caused by the calamity will be relieved when the slave thinks deeply about what Allah has bestowed on them as compared to what they have lost" (Al-Jawziyyah, 171) and what others have lost. If a person compared his or her state to others who are worse off, he or she will realize that his or her situation is not that bad and feel some relief. He finishes resting on the belief of the Hereafter where all anguish persons can find ease.

Al-Suyuti indicated prayer also enhances psychological well-being since it brings pleasure and comfort because prayer contains "the excellencies of this world and of the next" (1962, 159). It heals spiritual illnesses like greed, avarice, arrogance, and envy in this world and is an act honored by God.

After the 15th century, many of the works that were written on this issue were adding detail to the works that were already written. The foundation of Islamic healing was essentially established by the end of the 15th century; subsequent scholarly works explored these concepts in greater detail.

Recently, Muslims intellectuals have been inspired by Western scientific studies examining the efficacy of prayer and have begun to apply modern research methods to the field of Islamic healing.

Current research on prayer and healing

Five hundred university students in Konya (Turkey) completed a survey and majority (55%) reported that they performed the five daily *salat*, 27.2% reported that they performed *salat* occasionally, 8.2% reported praying once a week, and 8.4% never performed *salat*. Moreover, 40% of those who performed *salat* reported feeling happiness and comfort after the *salat* and 25.8% felt relieved because they felt their sins were forgiven (Sayin 2003, 96). In another research study (n = 150), a substantial number of patients (48.6%) reported that they experienced a positive emotional response (i.e., happiness) when they fulfill their religious obligations, and a number of patients (16.7%) reported that they felt happiness when supplicating (Kizmaz 1998, 45). Kizmaz noted that 200 verses in the Qur'an are about or related to *du'a*. Both studies were conducted in cities where larger segments of the population in the cities are practicing Muslims in comparison to other regions in Turkey. If they had been conducted in cities where the secular population was higher, results might have been different, though the degrees of difference have not been determined.

In another survey conducted in Turkey with 271 people, 95.4% of women and 94.3% of men expressed that they believed that *du'a* had positive effects. 86.2% of women and 85.1% of men stated that *du'a* was very important to them. 28% made *du'a* after prayer. 49.4% did not have a specific time for *du'as*. 15.6% prayed when they felt they needed it. 39.9% reported feeling closer to God when making *du'a*. 44.6% reported feeling peace and comfort when making *du'a*. 68.5% of women and 61.7% of men reported to have benefited from *du'a*. 16.2% of women and 11.4% of men said they occasionally benefited from *du'a*. 70.3% made *du'a* during depression. 17.9% would sometimes make *du'a* when depressed. 11.8% never made *du'a* during depression. 75.6% reported benefiting from *du'a* during depression. 20.9% reported to be uncertain. 3.5% reported not seeing its benefits. 47.6% would make *du'a* often to relieve stress. 33.9% made *du'a* sometimes to relieve stress. 8.9% reported making *du'a* rarely to relieve stress. 8.5% reported never making *du'a* during stress. 78.9% benefited from making *du'a* during difficult times. 19.2% reported to be undecided. 73.8% reported benefiting physically from *du'a* during illnesses. 22.3% reported not benefiting physically from *du'a* (Dogan 1997, 55-97).

Some scholars of Islam deemed congregational *salat* as group exercise and asserted that they benefit a person's morale and well-being. Al-Dhahabi posited that *salat* positively affects the body and soul (Rahman 1987, 44). According to Al-Jawziyyah, if a person is spiritually strong, *salat* will have a positive effect on that person psyche. He viewed *salat* as an exercise for the body and soul because it moves most parts of the body and decreases depression (1999, 109).

Adnan al-Tharshi investigated the relationship between prayer and healing and employed empirical methods. He found that prayer, which includes *salat*, *du'a*, recitation of Qur'an, *dhikr*, has physical, psychological and spiritual benefits (Al-Tharshi 1992, 6) For example, a person who performs the five daily *salat* performs around 280 varied body movements, including standing, bowing 36 times, prostrating 72 times, deep breathing, neck movements, raising the hands, moving the digits, and sitting (97-123). This can be considered as light exercise, which improves blood flow, works out the muscles, and decreases calcification. He quotes from Stirk and Balaskas (1979), pointing out that the movements of *salat* are similar to the yoga movements and exercises recommended to pregnant women (67-70).

In the last few decades, spiritual healing and physical exercises like yoga and reiki have attracted many enthusiasts and become one of the fastest growing health trends. In the *Journal of the Royal Society of Medicine*, yoga was found to have health benefits that "encompass body, mind, and spirit" (Wood 1993, 254-258). Al-Tharshi compares yoga positions to *salat* positions, showing that five positions in Islamic prayer, each having a corresponding position to yoga (1992, 116-142).

The Islamic prayer can provide the similar benefits of yoga to Muslims. Each position in prayer activates all seven *chakras*, energy fields, in the body. These correlate to the five major nerve ganglia in the spine. Because the different organs in the body are connected, moving one can affect the other. Studies point out that certain body movements can evoke emotional and physical responses, such as increased circulation after smiling. The *takbir*, raising hands to the level of the head, and *qiyam*, standing upright, together parallel the mountain pose in yoga, found to improve posture, balance, and self-awareness. Such movements help asthma and heart patients as it stabilizes blood pressure and breathing. *Ruku*, bending at ninety degree with the hands on the knees, is like the forward bend position in yoga; it stretches the muscles of the lower back, thighs, leg, calves, and allows for free circulation to the upper torso. It increases blood flow to the brain and lungs, improving brain function. The *julus*, sitting on both legs, firms he thighs, knees, and toes. Furthermore, it aids digestion, detoxification of the liver, and stimulates action in the intestine. This makes it necessary to perform the movements correctly (Al-Tharshi, 116-142).

He also mentions the work of cardiologist Ali Sabri Sayrafi at Al-Azhar University who attributes a long period of little or no exercise as one of the causal factors of heart attacks. *Salat*, he states, decreases the chances of heart attacks and benefits the circulatory system (Tharshi, 220). He cited research conducted by Tawfiq Alawan, who found fewer orthopedic problems in those who pray in comparison to those who don't pray. Also, those who pray have around 90% less calcification, the accumulation of calcium salts on body tissue which can lead to difficulty in moving joints (Tharshi, 239). Because of the frequency and regularity of prayer throughout one's life, prayer's influences on the body remain strong and consistent.

Sufism and healing

Sufism, the spiritual aspect of Islam dedicated to divine love, focuses on healing through *dhikr*, remembrance of God, and meditation. The Sufi method of healing uses spiritual power and has been practiced by Sufis for centuries, sometimes as a daily ritual. Their methods include meditation, *dhikr*, *tefekkur*, contemplation about the universe and the life hereafter, and other modes of disciplining the heart.

Sufism focuses on a person's inner dimension, including the emotions and spiritual strengths and weaknesses. Sufis see true healing as existential, attaining a state where the human body, mind, and heart functions harmoniously with the universe (Skeikh & Sheikh 1989, 166). This is based on the Sufi concept of connectedness to the universe and the entities within due to having the same Creator. This bridges the existence of all entities and put them into a relationship of coexistence and cooperation instead of conflict.

Dhikr is essential for Sufi healing. Under the supervision of a Sufi master, a person would invoke certain names of God on a daily basis.

This can be done by oneself or with a group. The group or person should make *dhikr* in a quiet and uncluttered room. The person would close his or her eyes, relax the body, and breathe deeply. First, he or she would think about death, then being in God's presence with his or her Sufi master. The person would then choose a certain name or names of God mentioned in the Qur'an and repeat them over. The length of this session depends on the individual or group. Some last as short as fifteen minutes while others can last over an hour.

Sufi thinker and philosopher, Al-Ghazali posits that healing requires a person to decrease or eliminate unhealthy passions and impressions on the psyche. Through this type of activity, a person creates healthy diversion from discomforting matters of the mind and heart (Araseth & Sheikh, 173). Jalal-ad-Din Muhammad Balkhi (1207-1273), know as Rumi in the West, a Muslim poet and Sufi leader, highlights inner conflicts as the source of all maladies; therefore, the cure must occur from within the individual (Nasr 1991, 174). The human psyche can remain healthy only when it is in quest of beloved God with whom is the goal of all mystical romances (32).

A similar method to the Sufi practice is recommended under current Western alternative healing by Herbert Benson, MD, Director Emeritus of Benson-Henry Institute, Mind-Body Medical Institute and Associate Professor of Medicine at Harvard Medical School. In *Timeless Healing* (1996), Benson states, "The brain seems to use the quiet time to wipe the slate clean so that new ideas and beliefs can present themselves.... a period of brain focusing to the exclusion of everyday thoughts can actually increase mental productivity" (138). His nine-step relaxation method also involves choosing a quiet room, breathing deeply, closing the eyes, repeating a word or phrase "firmly rooted in your belief system" for twenty minutes, and assuming a passive attitude by ignoring other thoughts that come (136).

Another study was conducted by psychologist Vander Hoven in Netherlands. He focused on the effects of reading the Qur'an and repeating the word "Allah" both on patients and non-patients. Not all patients were Muslims, and not all could speak Arabic, and had to learn to pronounce "Allah" clearly. The effects were more visible on those who suffered from tension. The psychologist told the Saudi daily *Al-Watan* that correct pronunciation of each letter in the word "Allah" has a different effect, from relaxing the aspiration and controlling the heart beat (from Qatari "Arraya", 24 March, 2002).

In my study, I asked the participant how often he or she contemplates about the universe, death, and the life Hereafter. *Dhikr* is a part of the prayer in my research, so I also employed *dhikr* in the sessions with the participants, although it is a much shorter session that the Sufi practice. The results of the short *dhikr* sessions with the other prayers are reviewed in the Research Findings section.

Western sources

The relationship between health and healing has been receiving more attention in the last four decades. It is not uncommon to find an article about prayer and healing in a medical journal. It is usually approached as an alternative therapy or a supplement to medical or psychological treatment. Most studies support the contention that prayer has positive effects. There have also been other studies that found that prayer had little or no effect (even negative effects) on physical well-being. I reviewed these studies. First, the principal investigator focused on the research describing positive effects.

Spirituality has become a subject of interest in the healthcare field since it was recognized to have the potential to heal. Scientific studies over the last four decades have examined the role of both public and private religious expression on health and longevity. As of 2003, «2,200 published reports, including books, articles, dissertations, abstracts, and other works on spiritual healing, energy medicine, and intentionality. This included 121 laboratory studies; 75 randomized, controlled trials; 128 summaries or reviews; 96 reports of observational studies and non-randomized trials; 276 descriptive studies, case reports, and surveys, 1,273 other writings including opinions, claims, anecdotes, letters to editors, commentaries, critiques, and meeting reports, and 264 selected books» (Jonas & Cawford 2003, 57).

Recently, the psychiatric profession has begun to explore the relation between spirituality and well-being; however this topic has been neglected because of a tendency toward materialistic reductionism (Cloninger 2006, 2).

Prayer and healing concern not only individual practitioners, but has been given attention at prominent organizations and research institutions. The Joint Commission on Accreditation of Healthcare Organizations (JCAHO) stated, «For many patients, pastoral care and other spiritual services are an integral part of health care and daily life. The hospital is able to provide for pastoral care and other spiritual services for patients who request them» (Puchalski 2001, 353). JCAHO requires that patients undergo spiritual assessment (Hodge 2006, 158). Other umbrella organizations of medical institutions and physicians support research exploring the relation between spirituality and health. Such institutions include the Association of American Medical Colleges, American College of Physicians, Harvard Medical School, Mayo Clinic, and Duke Clinical Research Institute.

Laboratories at Harvard Medical School established that when a person engages in repetitive prayer, word, sounds or phrases, and when intrusive thoughts are disregarded, a set of specific physiological changes ensue. There is decreased metabolism, heart rate, rate of breathing and slower brain waves (Benson 1996, 63-64).

Over five thousand members of an organization received surveys and a substantial subset (86 %) completed the survey. Almost half (47.5%) of those responding reported that they pray for their health and a substantial number of individuals (90.3%) employing prayer to achieve good health reported that they believed that prayer improved their health.

The subset reporting that they use prayer to achieve good health, more favorable health-related behaviors, preventive service use, and satisfaction with care (O'Connor, Pronk, Tan, & Whitebird 2005, 369-75).

Conducted by Ferraro and Albretch-Jensen, a national sample of non-institutionalized adults showed that respondents with frequent religious practices were associated with better health, regardless of age

(1991). In an analysis of 42 different studies and examination of 125, 826 people, McCullough found a correlation between participation in religion and increased life expectancy (Al-Kandari 2003, 465).

Jeff Levin, another leading figure in the study of spirituality and medicine, covered the topic of healing and faith in several books and articles. He concluded that prayer has positive effects on health and summarizes them in seven principles:

1. Religious affiliation and membership benefit health by promoting healthy behavior and lifestyle.

2. Regular religious fellowship benefits health by offering support that buffers the effects of stress and isolation.

3. Participation in worship and prayer benefits health through the psychological effects of positive emotions.

4. Religious beliefs benefit health by their similarity to health-promoting beliefs and personality styles.

5. Simple faith benefits health by leading to thoughts of hope, optimism, and positive expectation.

6. Mystical experiences benefit health by activating a healing bio-energy or life force or altered state of consciousness.

7. Absent prayer for others is capable of healing by paranormal or by divine intervention. (Levin 2001, 13)

Levin uses the term "theosomatic medicine"- literally, a model or view of the determinants of health based on the apparent connections between God, or spirit, and the body (2001, 163).

Another study reported a link between health and attendance of religious services. Those who did not attend religious services on a regular basis had 1.87 times the risk of death compared to those who did attend (Hummer et. al 1999, 273-285). An inverse relationship between the number of years of attending religious services and smoking was discovered in a study of 3,968 persons age 65 and older in North Carolina. Higher participation in religious activities at one wave predicted lower rates of smoking at future waves (Koenig 1998, 210). Since smoking is highly detrimental to health, a relationship between religious activity and better physical health may be associated with altered patterns of smoking behavior. In a similar study, frequent church attendees were noted to have stronger immune systems than less frequent attendees (1997, 246). Members in religious kibbutzim lived longer than those in secular kibbutzims, in spite of social support and conventional health behaviors (Kark et.al. 1996, 345).

There are many studies supporting the benefits of prayer. However, there are no clear regulations as to how to administer tests regarding prayer.

Insignificant negative effects

Although research efforts are much more likely to focus on the positive effects of prayer, negative effects have been observed, although they are fewer in comparison to the heavily researched positive effects.

Misunderstanding or ignorance of religious practices in healing can sometimes lead to negative consequences. Fatalistic thinking, use of amulets, and superstitious practices by individuals, including charlatans and some faith healers, carry a large potential for adverse psychological and physical consequences. For example, a person may use risky remedies or not seek medical treatment, and may associate their sicknesses with guilt and punishment (Ismail et. al. 2005, 26). However, it is not prayer per se, but rather theological misunderstanding of illness that causes health risks, such as not seeking medical treatment or relying on charlatans.

Fatalistic thinking

The doctrine of fatalism denies free will and leads to inaction and passive acceptance of events. Research has confirmed that fatalism is correlated with helplessness, hopelessness, anxious preoccupation, and cognitive avoidance (Cotton et. al. 1999, 429). In the Muslim world, fatalism arose from the misinterpretation and misunderstanding of the context of some Qur'anic verses, such as *"And you can not will (to do so) God will, the Lord of worlds"* (81:29). In order to correctly interpret a verse like this one, a person must have a deep understanding of Qur'an and Qur'anic sciences. Furthermore, without investigating the causes of their misfortunes, some Muslims accept whatever occurs as God's will. In the case of illnesses, they ignore preventive care and jeopardize their health, relying on prayers alone while denying the role of free will. Belief in God's will is a core principle of Islamic faith. However, "to assume this equates with fatalism and a passive attitude towards illness and health is oversimplistic" as research shows that such a belief did not prevent people from searching for causes for their illness or taking steps to seek a cure (Ismail et. al. 2005, 30).

Fatalistic thinking is contradictory to the Qur'anic verses and the *sunnah*, the tradition of Prophet Muhammad, peace be upon him, peace be upon him. In the Qur'an, it says, "... *and make not your own hands contribute to (your) destruction, but do good; for Allah loves those who do good*" (2:195). There are many *hadiths* regarding this topic. A few are written below:

> Prophet Muhammad, peace be upon him, was walking with his companions. Upon coming to an insecure wall, he sped past it. The companions told the Prophet, "Whatever is predestined will happen, so why are you running?" To which the Prophet replied, "It is my responsibility to save myself from hazard." (Canan 1993, 133)

> Treatment is also a part of predestination (132).

> When the Prophet heard that people in a certain village contracted a contagious disease, he ordered that the villagers stay in the village and outsiders stay outside, thus quarantining the sickness. The Prophet made seeking treatment obligatory on ill persons (Al-Jawziyyah 1999, 25)

Based on these verses and traditions of Prophet Muhammad, peace be upon him, Islamic scholars regard seeking treatment as an obligation physically and *sunnah* spiritually (Rahman 1987, 48).

> Usame bin Shuraik narrated that "I was with the Prophet when the Bedouins came to him and said 'O Messenger of Allah, should we seek medicine?' He said, 'Yes, O slave of Allah, seek medicine, for Allah has not created a disease except that he has also created it

cure, except for one illness.' They said "What was that?' He said 'Old age'" (Al-Jawziyyah 1999, 25).

Al-Dhahabi points out the command of Prophet Muhammad, peace be upon him, "Get medical treatment" as proof that seeking treatment is meritorious (Al-Dhahabi 1996, 103).

Fatalistic thinking is more common among the illiterate and less educated in Muslim communities. Yet it is not prayers in itself that causes harm, but the misunderstanding of predetermination that keeps the people from seeking proper medical treatment.

Amulets (ruqya) and talismans

Amulets and talismans are objects meant to bring protection and good luck. They can be found in many faith traditions and cultures. In the Muslim world, people who are uneducated or less educated about religion use amulets that may contain Qur'anic verses, prayers, and symbols. Some people will not seek out modern therapeutic interventions; rather, they will rely on the amulets as a source of healing and protection from the evil powers that cause harm.

Prophet Muhammad, peace be upon him, had, at first, forbidden all amulets for fear that they contained certain words that compromised the rigorous monotheism of Islam by invoking spirits and other powers besides God (Rahman 1987, 88). Subsequently, he allowed their use but only if their contents were verses or hadiths and the person expected healing from God and not from the amulet itself (Al-Jawziyyah 1999, 29). The verses or hadiths on the amulets can then be read as prayers. Again, the prayers in the amulets are not the source of negative results, but rather it is the reliance on amulets as possessing curative power that may lead to an adverse outcome.

Superstition and folk culture

Believing illnesses to be inflicted spiritually (e.g., through black magic, ill omens, and curses), some people turn to *du'a* as the only method of healing, rather than seeking physical treatment. An alternative method is seeking assistance and advice from charlatans, *pirs* (respected and knowledgeable elders residing in India), sheiks (Middle East), and hocas in Turkey and the Balkans (Adib 2004, 698). Unfortunately, most of these practitioners lack medical training, and some become involved in superstitious practices that contradict Islamic norms and values such as recommending the use of amulets. Some spiritual healing "experts" have used prayers and Qur'anic verses in their own healing practices, sometimes harming the patient physically. One example is the use of "blessed" water that contains printed Qur'anic verses or special prayers and may generate an intoxicating effect (701). Some healers even apply electric shocks to cure illness (Adib 2004, 699-701). Some non-practicing Muslims, who have little knowledge of or regard for Qur'anic injunctions and Prophetic statements in the medical sphere, also turn to superstitious practices alongside modern medicine.

In some Muslim countries, the tree nearest to a saint's grave is deemed to be sacred and holds the powers of the saint (Dafni 2006, 7). The ritual starts with a prayer to the saint, requesting spiritual intervention, and ends with tying a cloth to the tree. This practice does not benefit a person's health. Such practices are taken as Islamic. Muslim theologians and jurists classify these as bid'ah, innovation, while others go as far as calling them shirk, polytheism. In the Qur'an, some trees are used for God's oaths (Chapter 95), but this does not indicate that trees are sacred.

Another similar practice includes ascribing illness to the power of the evil eye, ill omens, and dark magic ranging from fortune-telling, *zar* ceremonies, and *sihr al-mahabba*, or love sorcery (Sengers 2003, 259-265). These are usually carried out with the use of *du'as* and other prayers.

Due to lack of healthcare and ignorance, some uneducated Muslims turn to charlatans or folk culture to cure the illness. Sengers *Women and Demons* (2003) provides ample detail about this choice of healing. Some of these alternative healers recommend the ill person to seek physical treatment, while others only offer prayers or make amulets.

At the other end of the spectrum, there are some non-practicing Muslims who prefer to rely completely on modern medicine. The vast majority of Muslims, however, fall somewhere between these two extremes. They believe that prayer, supplications, Qur'anic recitation, and *dhikr* (remembrance of Allah) play an important role in healing and recovery, but they also recognize the benefits of modern medicine (Yousif 2002, 5).

If modern medical treatments become more available and accessible to the poor and uneducated in the Muslim world, the reliance on cures through folk culture will decrease greatly.

SUMMARY

In this section, the principal investigator reviewed the literature focusing on the relation between prayer and healing theologically and empirically. I summarized the literature: the Qur'an and *sunnah* of Prophet Muhammad, peace be upon him, and historical and current Islamic sources. The themes important to this study from this review are:

1) it is *fard*, a religious obligation, for Muslims to seek proper medical treatment;
2) prayer is strongly recommended alongside physical treatment;
3) prayer has spiritual, physical, psychological, and emotional benefits;
4) prayer generally gives comfort and reduces fears and anxieties;
5) some people misunderstand the concept of prayer and healing in Islam and harm themselves through avoiding medical treatment or using uneducated and uncontrolled charlatans healing methods.

The relationship between prayer and healing needs further study. There are few empirical studies, specifically in the area of medicine. The physical effects of regular prayer are touched upon, but need further research in order to develop a strong theory. Further studies should use scientific methods to examine the effects of prayer on healing.

Chapter III

Methodology

METHODOLOGY

INTRODUCTION

This chapter explains the methodology used for this research study. This research was conducted at Brigham and Women's Hospital, a Harvard Medical School-affiliated institution in Boston, Massachusetts. The chapter includes the following subsections: 1) Research Design; 2) Participants; 3) Description of Sessions; 4) Data Analysis; and 5) Chapter Summary.

RESEARCH DESIGN

The goal of this research study is to investigate the physical and spiritual effects of prayer on Muslim patients. This was done by a preliminary (Appendix C) and post-test survey (Appendix F) and recording of vital signs by the principal investigator. The data was analyzed by a team, which includes the principal investigator, as well as Imam Talal Eid, ThD, Wayne M. Dinn, neuropsychological researcher, Burak Alptekin, MD.

Sixty adult Muslim inpatients were recruited from the patient population at Brigham and Women's Hospital (BWH). The principal investigator administered a demographic and preliminary self-assessment survey before the prayers and a post-test survey was completed after the prayers. The questions on the surveys were asked by the principal investigator.

The pre-test survey includes five demographic questions and 25 questions that assess the spiritual level of the patients. This was completed at the beginning of the first session. The post-test survey contains 19 questions and was completed after the prayers in each session. Both surveys were used to compare the patient's emotional and spiritual state before and after the prayer and control conditions.

The surveys were developed by the principal investigator in the light of Islamic sources. The Qur'an and *hadith* mention the attributes of a strong believer and spiritual person. These are general aspects of Islamic practices such as *salat* (prayer), *du'a* (supplication), *dhikr* (remembrance), fasting, congregational prayer, pursuit of religious knowledge, reading and recitation of Qur'an, contemplation of the Hereafter, and charity.

In the first session, the patient recited or read certain short chapters and verses of Qur'an, invocation, and supplication of Prophet Muhammad to the patient. If the patients desired or were unable to recite, the principle investigator recited the certain verses and prayers by their side. In the second session, a non-religious text was read to serve as a control to determine if the *du'as* were affecting the patient. The non-religious text was in Arabic, just like the *du'as* and invocations, but did not contain religious references. The selected texts were short stories written in a simpler Arabic meant for learners of the Arabic language.

These general aspects were chosen based on the books of Ibn al-Qayyim al-Jawziyyah (1291-1350), *Healing with the Medicine of the Prophet* (1999), Abu Hamid Muhammad ibn Muhammad Al-Ghazali (1050-1111), *Ihyay-I Ulumudden* (The Revival of Religious Science 1976), Said Nursi (1880-1960), *The Letters*, Fethullah Gülen, *Questions and Answers about Faith* (1993), and George S. Stavros, *An Empirical Study of the Impact of Contemplative Prayer on Psychological, Relational and Spiritual Wellbeing* (1997).

The patients' answers on the surveys were used to measure their level of religiosity and spirituality and emotional conditions before and after the test. The preliminary and post-test surveys have questions that can be separated into two categories: first; those that ask about open religious practices like *salat* (daily prayers), *sadaqah* (almsgiving), *sawm* (fasting), and other practices; second, those that ask about beliefs and emotions. Wayne M. Dinn, neuropsychological researcher, assisted with data analysis.

The spiritual condition of the patients was assessed by their responses to the survey questions and evaluated at the end of data collection by Imam Talal Eid, ThD., and by the principal investigator, independently of Imam Eid. Each patient's spiritual conditions before the recitation or readings of prayers and nonreligious texts were compared. The principal investigator finalized the spiritual evaluation based on both assessments and assigned each patient a number between zero and ten, with ten being the highest level of spirituality.

The surveys were used to determine the level of religiosity and spirituality, the effects of prayer, and the theological approach of the patient to spirituality and religion. The purpose of recording vital signs is to compare the patient's physical state before and after the prayer and control conditions, and determine whether there was an association between prayer and changes in the patient's physical state

The physical conditions of patients were monitored and recorded before and immediately after the prayer sessions by the principal investigator. The vital signs from the pre-test recording and post-test recording were compared. The recorded and compared vital signs were then examined by Burak Alptekin, M.D., at Beth Israel Deaconess Medical Center (BIDMC). He explained the significance of the differences in the comparisons.

This research followed the Health Insurance Portability and Accountability Act (HIPAA) regulations. The study was approved by the Institutional Review Board (IRB) of Boston University and by Partners Human Research Committee, an umbrella organization of thirteen health institutions in Massachusetts, including BWH. Potential participants were asked to read and sign the informed consent statement (Appendix B). To protect the privacy of participants, a numerical identification code was used for surveys and questionnaires.

Participants

The study was initiated after obtaining patient consent and permission from the health institution. Sixty adult Muslim inpatients ages 18-85

were recruited at Brigham and Women's Hospital (BWH). The participants who were recruited were part of my chaplain rounds at BWH. As
the Muslim chaplain, the principal investigator has access to the list of
patients who were recorded as Muslims patients upon their admission
to the hospital. The principal investigator visited these patients, and at
the end of the visit, the principal investigator told the patient about the
study. Patients who agreed to participate were asked to read and sign
the informed consent statement. The informed consent statement provides a description of the study design and how the principal investigator used information acquired during interactions with the participant.

DESCRIPTION OF SESSIONS

After the patient read and signed the consent statement, she or he
answered the demographics questions on the surveys that asked for
the patient's name, gender, age, marital status, and education. In
addition, the patient answered the survey questions designed to assess
the patient's level of religiosity and spirituality.

Before engaging in the prayer, vital signs were recorded by the
nurse or principal investigator. Vital signs included body temperature, blood pressure, and respiratory rate. The principal investigator
was trained to read and record vital signs by BWH staff.

The patient recited or read certain verses of Qur'an, invocation,
and supplication of Prophet Muhammad, peace be upon him, when he
or she desired. These verses, invocations, and supplications were selected from the *sunnah* of the Prophet related to healing. If the patient did
not want to or was not able to recite or read the Arabic prayers, the
principal investigator recited or read to the patient at the bedside. The
selection of verses, invocation, and supplication are listed below and
full texts are in Appendix D:

- The verses from the Qur'an are the entire chapters of *Al-Fati-
  ha*, the Opening (1:1-7), *Ayatul Kursi*, the Verses of the
  Throne (2:256), *Al-Falaq*, the Daybreak (113:1-5), *An-Naas*,
  Mankind (114:1-6).

- Invocations include *La ilaha illallah* (there is no god but God) 33 times. *Ya Shafi ya Allah* (O Healer, O God) will be said 33 times.
- The supplication of Prophet Muhammad, peace be upon him, for this study is *Allahumma inni asalukal afwa wal afiyata fiddunya wal akhira. Allahumma inni asalukal afwa wal afiyata fii deeni wa dunyaya wa ahli wa mali. Allahumma ashfii bi jahin nabiyyika salla Allahu alayhi wasallam.*

"O our Lord, I ask from you forgiveness and good health in this world and the Herafter. O our Lord, I ask forgiveness and safety in my religion and my life and my family and my possessions. O our Lord, heal me for the sake of Your Messenger, may God bless him."

After these prayers, vital signs were recorded again in each session. The first session lasted about 20 minutes in total.

The second session was conducted a few hours after the first session. In the second session, the patient read a non-religious text (see Appendix E) or let the principal investigator read if he or she wished. The text is a two-page story that does not consist of religious or spiritual references or religious teachings. This is the control condition that allowed the team to compare the patient's response to the religious and non-religious texts.

Two tests were performed daily for two to five days with several hours between each. Because the times of the sessions were dependant on the condition of the patient, there was no certain time for the sessions in general. If the prayer test was performed first, and the reading test was performed second on one day, then the next day, the reading test would be conducted first, and prayer test would be second.

DATA ANALYSIS

The recordings of vital signs were examined by Burak Alptekin, M.D. By comparing the pre-test and post-test vital signs recordings, he wrote whether the differences, if any, between pre-test and post-test conditions, were "positive", "negative", or "neutral".

Wayne M. Dinn, neuropsychological researcher, assisted with data analysis. He looked at the answers given to questions that did not ask about religious practice or spirituality. He compared patients' pre-test emotional conditions to post-test emotional conditions.

The patients' answers to survey questions were used to measure their level of religiosity and spirituality. At the end of the data collection, Imam Talal Eid, evaluated the responses and rated the patient's religious level based on the degree in which the patient fulfilled the *fard*, obligatory practices, *sunnah* of Prophet Muhammad, which are recommended practices, and the frequency of performing both practices. Since fard practices are a priority in Islam, they are given more importance in rating. Both Imam Eid and the principal investigator evaluated the survey. However, each of the evaluations was independently completed. After Imam Eid completed his evaluations, as the principal investigator, the principal investigator finalized the spiritual evaluation based on both assessments. When a there was a difference in the ratings, the mean number was chosen.

The principal investigator used the results from the team's analysis of the vital signs and surveys to write the results of his study on the effects of prayer on Muslim patients' well-being.

SUMMARY

This chapter explained the rationale behind the research design and survey questions. The questions that measured religiosity and spirituality were devised in light of the Qur'an, hadith, and scholarly books. The selected prayers were chosen by the recommendations of Prophet Muhammad and later influential scholars. Vital signs were employed to assess physical reactions. Three professionals were part of the research team to further investigate and understand the patient's conditions and the effects of prayer. This increases the accuracy of the research.

CHAPTER IV

Research Findings

RESEARCH FINDINGS

The fundamental question that guided this study was how prayer affected Muslim patients' well-being. In this chapter, the principal investigator presented the empirical findings, which include the results of preliminary surveys, post-test surveys, and vital sign recordings in detail. The Findings section has been split into two parts. The first part consists of graphs and percentages to display results for the surveys. This part is a basic data presentation geared towards ministers and divinity students. The second part consists of organized data, such as average ratings and standard deviation, and includes the vital signs, which are not included in the first part, presented in tables and histograms for the organized data. For this section, Statistical Package for the Social Sciences (SSPS) was used to organize and measure data for statistical purposes.

PART I

The participants

The principal investigator proposed participation to 68 adult Muslim in-patients to different units at Brigham and Women's Hospital in Boston, Massachusetts. 65 in-patients accepted to participate and signed the consent form (Appendix A). Three patients turned down participation. Five in-patients were discharged from the hospital before the minimum four trials were conducted. Coincidentally, there were an equal number of men and women. The patients' ages ranged from 18-84 with a mean age of 40.15.

76.6% (n=46) of patients were married, 11.6% (n=7) were single, 6.6% (n=4) were divorced, and 5% (n=3) were widowed.

One respondent had a PhD. 10% of participants (n=6) had a masters degree. 41.6% (n=25) had undergraduate degrees. 36.6% (n=22) had high school diplomas. 3.3% (n=2) completed up to middle school alone. 5% (n=3) completed elementary school alone. One respondent was illiterate. The mean educational level of the sample was 13.8 years (SD = 3.6).

Respondents comprised 25 nationalities. There were six Americans, six Pakistanis, six Somalians, five Turks, four Saudi Arabians, four Sudanese, and three Indians. The remaining 18 nationalities comprised of two or one person(s) each.

Out of 60 participants, 28.3% (n=17) were professionals, 15% (n=9) were blue collar workers, 11.6% (n=7) were retired, 8.3% (n=5) were students, and 36.6% (n=22) were housewives or women on maternity leave.

Patients were afflicted with a broad spectrum of conditions including cancer, cardiac disease, obstetrical conditions, orthopedic disease, and patients undergoing surgical procedures. A preliminary survey was used to determine the patients' level of religiosity or spirituality (from an Islamic perspective). The preliminary survey was also used to assess the intensity of depressive and anxiety symptoms as well as related variables reflecting the patient's emotional well-being (such as the degree of despair and loneliness).

All patients provided written informed consent. The Institutional Review Board at Boston University and the Partners Human Research Committee approved the study.

Results of the preliminary surveys

The purpose of the preliminary survey was to evaluate the religious, spiritual, and emotional conditions of the participant. It consisted of 25 questions: 17 asked the participant to respond in terms of a rating of zero through ten, five required a "yes" or "no" answer, and three were multiple-choice. Answers are based on verbal responses to the principal investigator who asked the questions.

1. Rate your level of depression (0 is not depressed and 10 is most depressed)

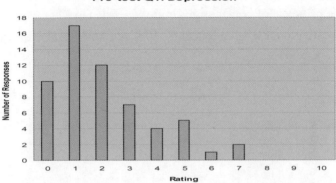

Out of 60 patients, 28.3% gave a rating of 1 for depression, 20% gave a rating of 2, 16.6% gave a rating of 0, 11.6% gave a rating of 3, 8.3% gave a rating of 5, 6.6% gave a rating of 4, 3.3% gave a rating of 7, 1.6% gave a rating of 6, and 3.3% did not respond to the question.

2. Rate your level of anxiousness (0 is not anxious and 10 is most anxious)

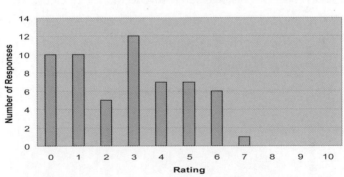

Out of 60 respondents, 20% gave a rating of 3, 16.6% gave a rating of 1, 15% gave a rating of 0, 13.3% gave a rating of 4, 11.6% gave rating of 5, 10% gave a rating of 6, 8.3% gave a rating of 2, 3.3% gave a rating of 7, 1.6% did not respond to the question/

3. Rate your level of anger towards God (Yes or No)

85% responded "No", 8.3% responded "Yes", and 6.6% did not respond. The high percentage of "No" responses may result from the Islamic principle of constant gratitude towards God.

4. Rate your level of loneliness (0 is not lonely and 10 is extremely lonely)

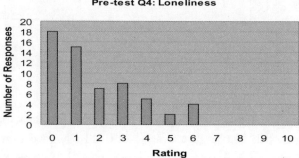

30% gave a rating of 0, 25% gave a rating of 1, 13.3% gave a rating of 3, 11.6% gave a rating of 2, 8.3% gave a rating of 4, 6.6% gave a rating of 6, 3.3% gave a rating of 5, and 1.3% did not respond.

5. Do you see yourself as submissive to the will of God? (Yes or No)

85% responded "Yes", 11.6% said "No", and 3.3% did not respond.

6. Rate your level of hopefulness (0 is not hopeful and 10 is extremely hopeful)

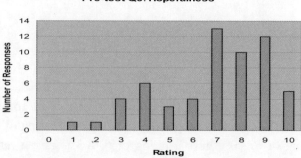

21.6% gave a rating of 7, 20% gave a rating of 9, 16.6% gave a rating of 8, 10% gave a rating of 4, 8.3% gave a rating of 10, 6.6% gave a rating of 6, 6.6% gave a rating of 3, 5% gave a rating of 5, 1.6% gave a rating 2, 1.6% gave a rating of 1, and 6.6% did not respond.

7. Rate your level of despair (0 is not despairing and 10 is having extreme despair).

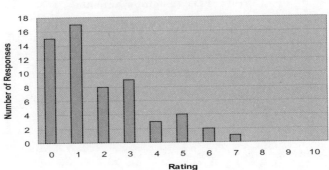

28.3% gave a rating of 1, 25% gave a rating of 0, 15% gave a rating of 3, 13.3% gave a rating of 2, 6.6% gave a rating of 5, 5% gave a rating of 4, 3.3% gave a rating of 6, 1.3% gave a rating of 9, and 1.3% did not respond.

8. Rate your level of confidence (0 is not confident and 10 is extremely confident).

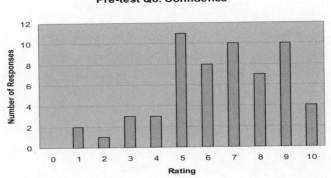

18.3% gave a rating of 5, 16.6% gave a rating of 9, 16.6% gave a rating of 7, 13.3% gave a rating of 6, 11.6% gave a rating of 8, 6.6% gave a rating of 10, 5% gave a rating of 4, 5% gave a rating of 3, 3.3% gave a rating of 1, 1.3% gave a rating of 2.

9. Rate your level of participation in religious activities in a week (0 is no participation and 10 is very active participation)

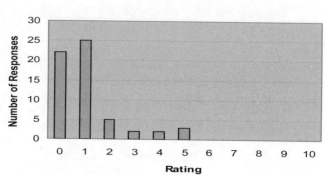

41.5% gave a rating of 1, 36.6% gave a rating of 0, 8.3% gave a rating of 2, 5% gave a rating of 5, 3.3% gave a rating of 4, 3.3% gave a rating of 3, and 1.6% did not respond.

10. Rate how often you consult a spiritual guide or mentor in a month (0 is no consulting and 10 is often consulting)

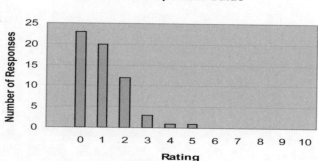

38.3% gave a rating of 0, 33.3% gave a rating of 1, 20% gave a rating of 2, 5% gave a rating of 3, 1.3% gave a rating of 4, and 1.3% gave a rating of 5.

11. Rate how important religion is to your life (0 is not important and 10 is extremely important)

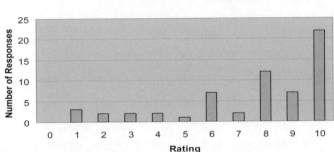

Pre-test Q11:Importance of Religion

36.6% gave a rating of 10, 20% gave a rating of 8, 15% gave a rating of 9, 11.6% gave a rating of 6, 5% gave a rating of 1, 3.3% gave a rating of 7, 3.3% gave a rating of 4, 3.3% gave a rating of 3, 3.3% gave a rating of 2, and 1.3% gave a rating of 1.

12. Rate how often you remember God (0 is never remembering God and 10 is always remembering God)

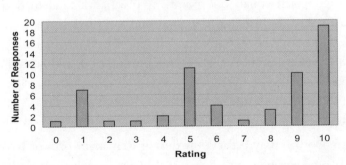

Pre-test Q12: Remembering God

31.6% gave a rating of 10, 18.3% gave a rating of 5, 16.6% gave a rating of 9, 11.6% gave a rating of 1, 6.6% gave a rating of

6, 5% gave a rating of 8, 3.3% gave a rating of 4, 1.3% gave a rating of 3, 1.3% gave a rating of 7, 1.3% gave a rating of 2, and 1.3% did not respond.

13. When do you pray (du'a)? (Check all that apply)
    a) During difficult times
    b) To express gratitude
    c) During Ramadan
    d) Fridays
    e) A few times a day
    f) Never
    g) Other _____

Pre-test Q13: Du'a

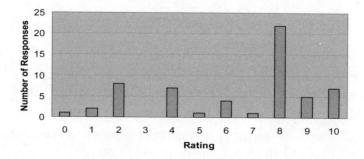

Each selected answer is worth 2 points, with the exception of choice g, which equals one point. 36.6% had a total of 8, 13.3% had a total of 2, 11.6% had a total of 10, 11.6% had a total of 4, 8.3% had a total of 9, 6.6% had a total of 6, 3.3% had a rating of 1, 1.3% had a rating of 7, 1.3% had a rating of 0, and 3.3% did not respond.

14. Do you pray (salat) five times a day? (Yes or No.)
    51.6% responded "Yes" and 48.3% responded "No".

15. Do you pray (salat) only during Ramadan? (Yes or No)
    71.6% responded "Yes" and 28.3% gave a rating of "No".

16. How many days do you fast in Ramadan? (Rate 1-30 days, or "can't fast")

Pre-test Q16: Days of Fasting

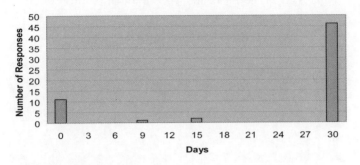

76.6% fasts for 30 days, 18.3% does not fast, 3.3% fasted for 15 days, and 1.3% fasted 9 days.

17. Do you go to mosque for prayer (salat) on a weekly basis (Yes or No)

53.3% responded "Yes" and 46.6% gave a response of "No".

18. How do you classify yourself as a Muslim?
    a) Religious (8-10)
    b) Spiritual (6-7)
    c) Sometimes practicing (3-5)
    d) Non practicing (0-1)

Pre-test Q18: Classification

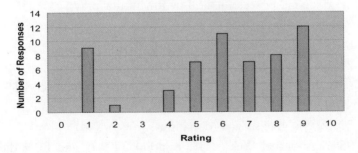

20% gave a rating of 9, 18.3% gave a rating of 6, 15% gave a rating of 1, 13.3% gave a rating of 8, 11.6% gave a rating of 7, 11.6% gave a rating of 5, 5% gave a rating of 4, 5% gave a rating of 0, 3.3% did not respond, and 1.3% gave a rating of 3.

19. Rate how much comfort you feel when you pray and make dua (0 is no comfort and 10 is a lot of comfort)

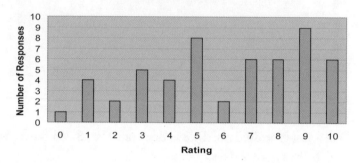

15% gave a rating of 9, 13.3% gave a rating of 5, 10% gave a rating of 10, 10% gave a rating of 8, 10% gave a rating of 7, 10% did not respond, 8.3% gave a rating of 3, 6.6% gave a rating of 4, 6.6% gave a rating of 1, 3.3% gave a rating of 6, 3.3% gave a rating of 2, and1.3% gave a rating of 0/

20. When you or someone from your family gets sick:
   a) You seek medical treatment only.
   b) You seek medical treatment and pray
   c) Pray only
   d) Neither seek medical treatment nor pray
   e) Other _____

85% responded b and 15% responded a.

21. Do you give zakat (alms)? (Yes or No)

65% responded "Yes", 33.3% responded "No", and 1.3% did not respond.

22. So you give sadaqa (donations) (Yes or No)

95% responded "Yes", 1.3% responded "No", and 1.3% did not respond.

23. How often do you give sadaqa?
   a) once a week
   b) once a month

c) quarterly
d) other _____

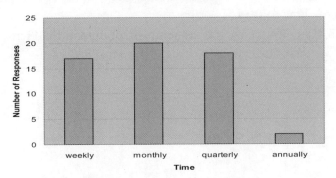

Pre-test Q23: Sadaqa

33.3% answered b, 60% answered c, 56.6% answered a, 5% did not respond, 3.3% answered d.

24. How often do you read the Qur'an or religious books? (0 is never and 10 is daily).
a) Daily (8-10)
b) Few times a week (5-7)
c) Weekly (2-4)
d) Monthly (1)
e) Never (0)
f) Other (i.e. can't read Arabic) _____

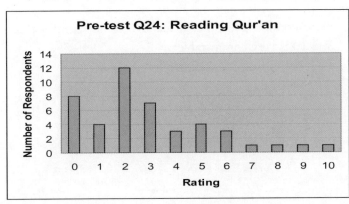

Pre-test Q24: Reading Qur'an

20% gave a rating of 2, 11.6% gave a rating of 3, 13.3% gave a rating of 0, 5% gave a rating of 4, 6.6% gave a rating of 5, 5% gave a rating of 6, 1.3% gave a rating of 7, 1.3% gave a rating of 8, 1.3% gave a rating of 9, 1.3% gave a rating of 10 and over, and 25% do not know how to read.

25. Rate how often you contemplate death and the Hereafter on a daily basis (0 is never and 10 is very often)

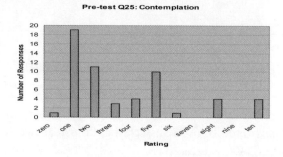

Pre-test Q25: Contemplation

31.6% gave a rating of 1, 18.3% gave a rating of 2, 16.6% gave a rating of 5, 6.6% gave a rating of 10, 6.6% gave a rating of 8, 6.6% gave a rating of 4, 6.6% did not respond, 5% gave a rating of 3, and 1.3% gave a rating of 6.

Results of religious post-test surveys

1. Do you feel more comfort after the prayer? (Yes or No)

83.3% responded Yes, 6.6% responded No, and 10% did not respond.

2. How comfortable do you feel? (0 is not comfortable at all and 10 is very comfortable)

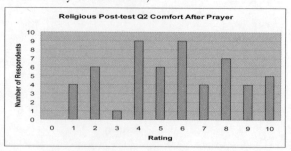

Religious Post-test Q2 Comfort After Prayer

6% gave a rating of 1, 10% gave a rating of 2, 1.6 % gave a rating of 3, 15% gave a rating of 4, 10% gave a rating of 5, 15% gave a rating of 6, 6% gave a rating of 7, 11.6% gave a rating of 8, 6% gave a rating of 9, 8.3% gave a rating of 10, and 8.3% did not respond.

3. Do you feel spiritually stronger after the prayer? (Yes or No)

78.3% responded Yes, 16.6% responded No, and 5% did not respond.

4. How strong do you feel spiritually? (O is not strong at all and 10 is very strong)

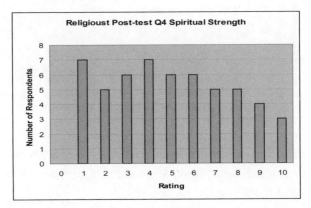

11.6% gave a rating of 1, 8.3% gave a rating of 2, 10% gave a rating of 3, 11.6% gave a rating of 4, 10% gave a rating of 5, 10% gave a rating of 6, 8.3% gave a rating of 7, 8.3% gave a rating of 8, 6% gave a rating of 9, 5% gave a rating of 10, and 10% did not respond.

5. How clear is your mind? (0 is not clear at all and 10 is very clear)

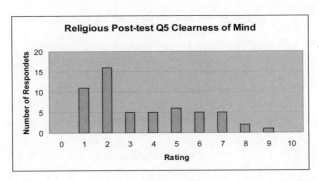

18.3% gave a rating of 1, 26.6% gave a rating of 2, 8.3% gave a rating of 3, 8.3% gave a rating of 4, 10% gave a rating of 5, 8.3% gave a rating of 6, 8.3% gave a rating of 7, 3.3% gave a rating of 8, 1.6% gave a rating of 9, and 6% did not respond.

6. How often would you like an imam to come and pray for you on a weekly basis? (O is never, 1 is once, and 10 is ten times a week)

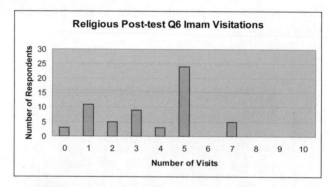

5% wanted no visits, 18.3% wanted one visit, 8.3% wanted two visits, 15% wanted three visits, 5% wanted four visits, 40% wanted five visits, and 8.3% wanted seven visits.

7. Would you like your family and friends to pray for you? (Yes or No)

90% responded Yes, 1.6% responded No, and 8.3% did not respond.

8. How often would you like your family and friends to pray for you? (0 is never, 1 is once a week, and 10 is ten times a week)

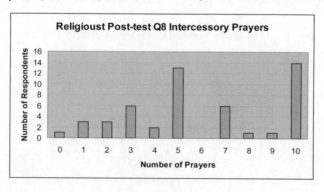

21.6% would like others to pray for them five times a day, 10% said seven times a day, 1.6% eight times a day, 1.6% nine times a day, 23.3% ten times a day, and 16% did not respond.

9. Do you feel closer to God after prayer? (Yes or No) 80% responded Yes, 13.3% responded No, and 8.3% did not respond.

10. Would you pray for people who you know are ill? (Yes or No) 88.3% responded Yes, 5% responded No, and 8.3% did not respond.

11. Do you feel God's presence after prayer? (Yes or No) 83.3% responded Yes, 8.3% responded No, and 8.3% did not respond.

12. Does *prayer affect* your physical condition? (Yes or No) 55% responded Yes, 33.3% responded No, and 11.6% did not respond.

13. Do you believe that prayer affects you positively? (Yes or No) 78.3% responded Yes, 15% responded No, and 6.6% did not respond.

14. Has praying increased your reliance upon God? (Yes or No) 80% responded Yes, 11.6% responded No, and 8.3% did not respond.

15. Would you recommend prayer to another patient? (Yes or No) 81.6% responded Yes, 11.6% responded No, and 8.3% did not respond.

16. If the imam does not come, will you pray or read Qur'an by yourself? (Yes or No) 68.3% responded Yes, 6.6% responded No, 25% can not read the Arabic Qur'an, and 8.3% did not respond.

17. How often do you pray (salat) daily? (0 is never and 10 is ten times a day) 50% does not pray daily, 5% prays three times a day, 1.6% prays four times a day, and 43.3% prays five times a day.

18. How many pages of Qur'an do you read or recite in a day? (0 is never and 10 is ten pages a day?

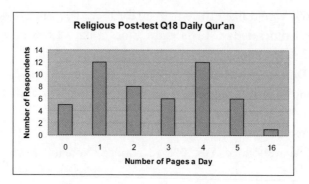

8.3% do not read any Qur'an, 20% read one page a day, 13.3% read two pages a day, 10% read three pages a day, 20% read four pages a day, 10% read five pages a day, 1.6% reads 16 pages a day, and 10% did not respond.

19. Will you continue to pray and recite Qur'an after you are discharged? (Yes or No)

90% responded Yes, 3.3% responded No, and 6.6% did not respond.

Results of non-religious post-test survey

1. Do you feel more comfort after the non-religious text reading? (Yes or No)

86.6% said No, 1.6% said yes, 8.3% did not respond.

2. How comfortable do you feel? (0 is not comfortable at all and 10 is very comfortable)

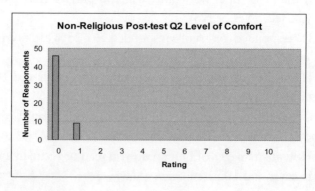

76.6% reported not feeling any difference after the reading, 15% reported feeling a little more comfortable and gave a rating of 1, and 3.3% did not respond.

3. Do you feel spiritually stronger after the non-religious text reading? (Yes or No)

5% replied Yes, 85% replied No, and 10% were not responsive.

4. How strong do you feel spiritually? (0 is not any different spiritually at all and 10 is very spiritual)

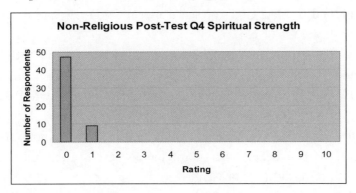

78.3% said they did not feel any spiritually stronger and gave a rating of 0, 15% gave a rating of 1, and 6.6% did not respond.

5. How clear is your mind? (0 is not clear at all and 10 is very clear)

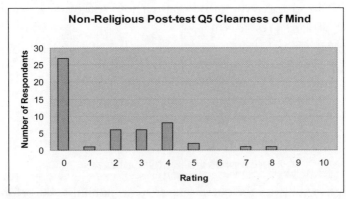

45% gave a rating of 0, indicating that nothing had changed, 1.6% gave a rating of 1, 10% gave a rating of 2, 10% gave a rating of 3, 13.3% gave a rating of 4, 3.3% gave a rating of 5, 1.6% gave a rating of 7, 1.6% gave a rating of 8, and 10% did not respond.

Questions 6-8, 10, 15-18 are already answered in the religious post-test survey and are not relevant to the non-religious reading.

9. Do you feel closer to God after non-religious text reading? (Yes or No)

3.6% responded Yes, 88.3% responded No, and 6.6% did not respond.

11. Did you feel God's presence after the non-religious text reading? (Yes or No)

13.3% responded Yes, 78.3% responded No, and 8.3% did not respond.

12. Does non-religious text reading affect your physical condition? (Yes or No)

0% responded Yes, 85% responded No, and 15% did not respond.

13. Do you believe that non-religious text reading affects you positively? (Yes or No)

3.3% responded Yes, 90% responded No, and 3.3% did not respond.

14. Has praying increased your reliance upon God? (Yes or No)

10% responded Yes, 85% responded No, and 5% did not respond.

19. Would you recommend non-religious text reading to another patient? (Yes or No)

1.3% responded Yes, 88.3% responded No, and 5% did not respond.

Part II

Descriptive statistics for preliminary and post-protocol questionnaires

Descriptive statistics for questionnaire items administered before the patient participated in the experimental and control protocols are presented in Table 1 (i.e., the preliminary survey).

Table 1
Demographic and Preliminary Survey Data

	Mean	Median	SD	Min.– Max.
Age	40.1	35.0	16.2	18 - 84
Educational Level	13.8	16.0	3.6	0 - 22
Religiosity/Spirituality	52.1	58.0	19.1	2 - 69
Depression	2.01	1.5	1.8	0 - 7
Anxiety	2.81	3.0	2.0	0 - 7
Loneliness	1.81	1.0	1.8	0 - 6
Hopefulness	6.89	7.0	2.26	1 - 10
Despair	1.91	1.0	1.92	0 - 9
Confidence	6.50	7.0	2.24	1 - 10
Comfort	6.05	6.5	2.83	0 - 10
Dua	6.45	8.0	2.85	0 - 10
Fasting	24.4	30.0	11.25	0 - 30
Remembrance	6.76	8.0	3.21	0 - 10
Importance	7.81	8.5	2.55	1 - 10
Classification	5.93	6.0	2.65	1 - 9

Descriptive statistics for questionnaire items administered after the patient participated in the prayer session or the control condition (i.e., non-religious text) are shown in Tables 2 (p.84) and 3 (p.90) (i.e., the post-experimental manipulation questionnaire).

Correlational analysis

Since response patterns on both questionnaires were frequently skewed, a nonparametric test (Spearman's rho) was used. First, specific items from the preliminary survey were combined to create a composite religiosity score. Correlational analysis revealed that religiosity/ spirituality index scores correlated negatively with scores on the depression and anxiety dimensions (Spearman's rho = -.38, $p < .003$ and Spearman's rho = -.55, $p < .000$). That is, higher scores on the religiosity/spirituality index were associated with lower depression and anxiety scores. Similarly, religiosity/spirituality index scores correlated negatively with scores on items assessing loneliness and despair, with Spearman's rho = -.37, p < .004 and Spearman's rho = -.23, p = .08, respectively. Although, the latter association did not reach statistical significance, the relationship was in the expected direction. Elevated religiosity/spirituality (as determined by self-report) scores were associated with lower scores on items measuring the patient's sense of despair and loneliness. Moreover, a positive relationship between self-reported religiosity and hopefulness / confidence was noted (Spearman's rho = .35, p < .007, and Spearman's rho = .42, p < .001). A greater degree of religiosity/spirituality was associated with hopefulness and confidence. All but the correlation between religiosity/spirituality and loneliness/despair of the aforementioned relationships were statistically significant. Finally, patients were asked to quantify the amount of comfort they experience following prayer (*salat*), supplication (*du'a*), and remembrance (*dhikr*). Not surprisingly, religiosity/spirituality scores were strongly associated with the level of comfort derived from *salat*, *du'a*, and *dhikr* (Spearman's rho = .57, p < .000).

Prayer and non-religious text conditions

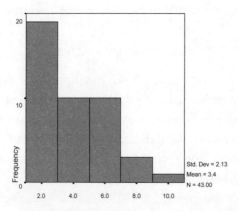

Mental Clarity After Prayer (0 = very clear; 10 = not at all clear)

Since response patterns on both prayer and non-religious text conditions questionnaires were frequently skewed (see Figure 1 for example: clarity of mind following prayer session with 0 = "very clear" and 10 = "not clear at all"), a nonparametric equivalent (Wilcoxon Signed Ranks Test) of the paired t-test was used for continuous data (ratings). To analyze patients' response patterns on dichotomous variables (yes/no responses), a nonparametric test (McNemar Test) was also employed.

Continuous variables

First, questions were combined to create a composite religiosity/spirituality score. Scores on the self-report measures were then compared (i.e., the post-experimental manipulation questionnaires administered after the patient participated in the prayer session and after the patient participated in the control session). Thus, each patient served as his or her own control. That is, each patient's score on the religiosity questionnaire administered after the prayer condition was compared to the patient's score on the questionnaire completed after the patient participated in the control non-religious reading. To eliminate order effects, patients were randomly assigned to prayer or non-religious control conditions. If the patients participated in the prayer protocol during session 1, he or she participated in the control protocol during session 2. If the patient participated in the control condition session 1, he or she listened to the reading of the non-religious text (control condition) during session 2. Note that two patients were discharged before completing the study and did not complete both questionnaires. Therefore, they were excluded from analyses that appear below.

Level of religiosity following prayer session and non-religious text condition

As shown in Table 2, after participating in the prayer session patients obtained significantly higher scores on a self-report measure of religiosity/spirituality in comparison to scores on the measure administered after the control condition (i.e., listening to the PI read from a non-religious text) ($p < .000$). Test differences were striking. As noted above, the Wilcoxon Signed Ranks Test was used to compare scores on the religiosity measure administered after the prayer session and the non-religious text control condition.

Table 2
Prayer and non-religious text conditions
Continuous Data: Mean Score and Standard Deviation

	Prayer		Non-religious Text	
	Mean	(SD)	Mean	(SD)
Religiosity/Spirituality Score	22.87	(8.82)	14.80	(6.35)
Degree of Comfort	5.10	(2.87)	0.17	(0.42)
Spiritual Strength	4.39	(2.75)	0.35	(0.58)
Mental Clarity	3.37	(2.12)	2.80	(1.30)
Visits from Imam	4.12	(2.16)	3.58	(2.07)
Prayer: Family/Friends	6.32	(2.83)	5.64	(2.94)
Daily Prayer	3.29	(2.45)	2.92	(2.24)
Qur'an	2.44	(2.78)	1.69	(1.36)

As Table 2 illustrates, patients participating in the prayer session reported that they experienced a greater degree of spiritual comfort and strength ($ps <. 000$). Moreover, they indicate a greater willingness to meet with an Imam following the prayer session in comparison to their interest in meeting with a Muslim chaplain following the control condition ($p < .01$) (i.e., "How often would you like an Imam to come and pray for you on a weekly basis? 0 is never; 1 is once a week; and 10 is ten times a week"). Interestingly, patients did not report a significantly greater degree of mental clarity following the prayer session in comparison to their level of clarity following the control condition ($p = .165$). In fact, patients reported a greater degree of clarity following the control condition; of course, as noted above, this difference did not approach statistical significance. Similarly, the prayer condition was not associated with a significantly greater interest in having friends/family offer prayers ($p = .46$) or an increase in the amount of recitation planned (i.e, reading the Qur'an) ($p = .19$); although differences were in the expected direction. Moreover, the intended daily prayer rate did not vary as a function of the experimental condition (i.e., following exposure to prayer or non-religious text) ($p = .27$). That is, patients reported that they were not significantly more likely to pray after participating in the prayer session in comparison to the non-prayer control condition.

Histograms: continuous data

The following histograms chart the results of the questions with multiple answers. The left column has the results for the prayer sessions (religious), and the right column has the results for the non-religious text session. The scores can be found in Table 2 (p.83).

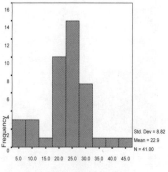

After Prayer: Religiosity/Spirituality Index

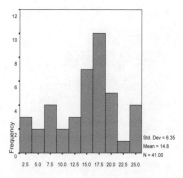

After Non-religious Text: Religiosity/Spirituality Index

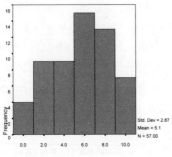

Comfort After Hearing Prayer

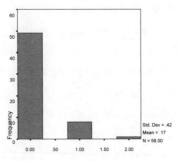

Comfort After Hearing Non-religious Text

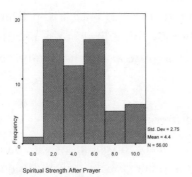

Spiritual Strength After Prayer

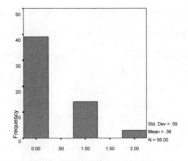

Spiritual Strength After Hearing Non-religious Text

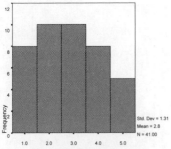

Mental Clarity After Non-religious Text

Mental Clarity After Prayer (0 = very clear; 10 = not at all clear)

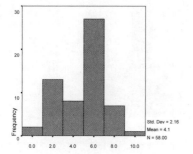

After Prayer: Visits by Imam (0 = never - 10 times per week)

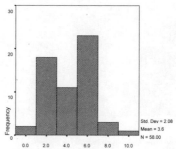

After Non-religious Text: Visits by Imam (0 = never - 10 times per week)

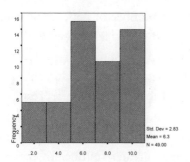

After Prayer: Desire to Have Friends/Family Pray (0 = Never)

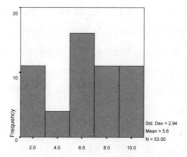

After Non-religious Text: Desire to Have Friends/Family Pray

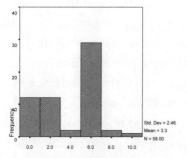

After Prayer: Frequency of Daily Prayer (intention) (0 = not at all)

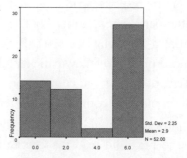

After Non-Religious Text: Frequency of Daily Prayer (intention)

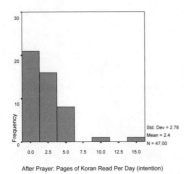

After Prayer: Pages of Koran Read Per Day (intention)

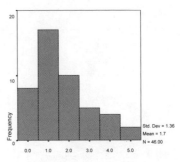

After Non-Religious Text: Pages of Koran Read Per Day (intention)

Dichotomous variables

A number of items produced dichotomous data (yes/no responses). As shown in Table 3, a significantly greater number of patients reported an alteration in their relationship to God (i.e., "felt closer to God") following the prayer session. In contrast, few subjects reported that they experienced an alternation in their relationship with God after participating in the control condition (see Table 3) (McNemar Test, $p <$ .000). Similarly, a significantly greater number of patients reported "feeling the presence of God" (McNemar Test, $p <$ .000) following the prayer session. Moreover, a substantially greater number of patients reported that prayer had a positive impact (McNemar Test, $p <$ .000), improved their physical condition ($p <$ .000), and that they had increased their reliance on God (McNemar Test, $p <$ .000) (in comparison to response patterns on the self-evaluation measure completed after participating in the control condition, i.e., listening to the PI read from a non-religious text). Patients were also more likely to recommend prayer to fellow patients following the prayer session (McNemar Test, p < .000) (in comparison to response patterns on the self-evaluation measure completed after the control condition).

A substantial number of patients reported that they would continue to pray and read the Qur'an following the prayer session *and* following the nonreligious control condition (see Table 3). Indeed, all of the patients reported that they would continue to pray and/or read the

Qur'an after hearing the nonreligious reading, while a substantial number of patients (approximately 96 %) reported that they would continue to pray and/or read the Qur'an after participating in the prayer session (condition differences did not approach significance since almost all of the patients reported a willingness to continue to pray/read the Qur'an following both conditions). Similarly, almost all of the patients reported that they will pray for others and would like others (i.e., family and friends) to pray for them after participating in the prayer and control conditions.

Table 3
Prayer and non-religious text conditions
Dichotomous Data: Yes/No Response

	Prayer	*Non-religious Text*
	Yes / No	**Yes / No**
Comfort	50 / 4	1 / 52
Spiritual Strength	47 / 10	3 / 51
Closer to God	48 / 8	2 / 53
Family /Friends	54 / 1	54 / 0
Intercessory Prayer	53 / 3	48 / 7
Presence of God	50 / 5	8 / 47
Impact on Physical Condition	25 / 21	0 / 51
Positive Influence	47 / 9	6 / 51
Increased Reliance Upon God	48 / 7	4 / 50
Recommend Prayer or Text	49 / 7	23 / 33
Koran	41 / 4	35 / 7
Continue to Pray/Read Koran	54 / 2	51 / 0

Prayer and Healing in Islam

Bar charts: *dichotomous data*

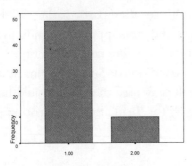

Spiritual Strength After Prayer: Yes = 1, No = 2

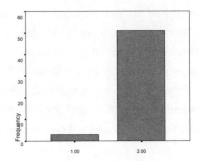

Spiritual Strength After Non-religious Text: Yes = 1; No = 2

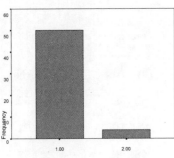

Comfort After Hearing Prayer: Yes = 1; No = 2

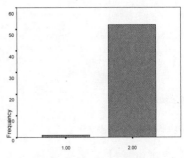

Comfort After Hearing Non-religious Text: Yes = 1; No = 2

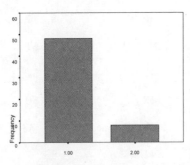

Closer to God After Prayer: Yes = 1; No = 2

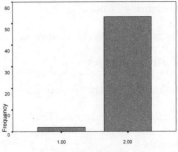

Closer to God After Non-religious Text: Yes = 1; No = 2

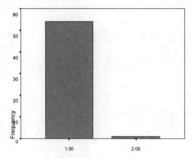

After Prayer: Family/Friends Pray for Patient: Yes = 1; No = 2

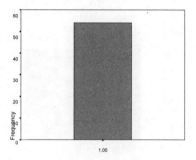

After Non-relig. Text: Family/Friends Pray for Patient: Yes = 1

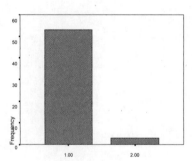

After Prayer Session: Intercessory Prayer: Yes = 1; No = 2

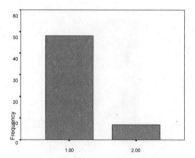

After Non-relig. Text--Intercessory Prayer: Yes = 1; No = 2

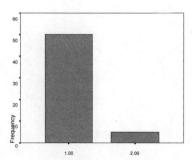

After Prayer--God's Presence: Yes = 1; No = 2

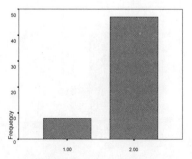

After Non-religious Text--God's Presence: Yes = 1; No = 2

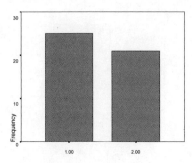

Prayer--Impact on Physical Health: Yes = 1; No = 2

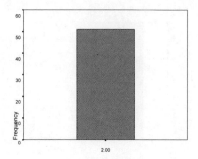

Non-Relgious Text--Impact on Physcial Health: No = 2

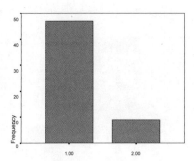

Positive Impact of Prayer: Yes = 1; No = 2

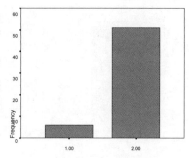

Positive Impact of Non-religious Text: Yes = 1; No = 2

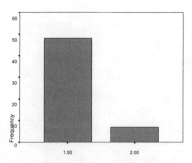

After Prayer--Increased Reliance Upon God: Yes = 1; No = 2

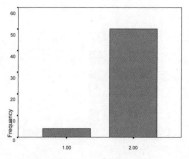

After Non-relig. Text--Reliance Upon God: Yes = 1; No = 2

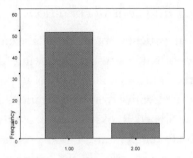

Recommend this Prayer: Yes = 1; No = 2

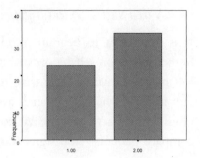

Recommend Non-religious Text: Yes = 1; No = 2

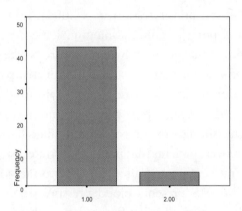

After Prayer--Continue to Read Koran: Yes = 1; No = 2

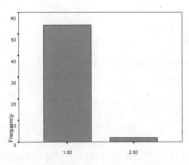

After Prayer--Continue to Pray and Recite: Yes = 1; No = 2

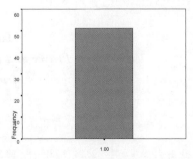

After Non-Relig. Text--Continue to Pray and Recite: Yes = 1

Vital signs following prayer and control conditions

It is important to bear in mind that patients obtained significantly higher scores on self-report measures of religiosity and well-being following the prayer session than to the control condition. It is important to note whether prayer is associated with favorable alterations in physiological activity. The Wilcoxon Signed Ranks Test was used to compare patients' vital signs (i.e, body temperature, blood pressure, and respiratory rate) before and after participating in the prayer and non-religious text sessions. As shown in Table 4, patients demonstrated a statistically significant increase in body temperature following participation in the prayer session ($p < .004$); however, alterations were subtle and not clinically meaningful. Patients' did not demonstrate a significant change in body temperature before and after exposure to the non-religious text ($p = .393$). Similarly, patients exhibited a statistically significant rise in respiratory rate following the prayer session ($p < .01$). Again, pre- and post-prayer session differences were subtle and should not be considered clinically meaningful (see Table 4). Moreover, patients' did not demonstrate a significant change in respiratory rate before and after exposure to the non-religious text ($p = .398$). Table 5 presents blood pressure data. Again, patients demonstrated a statistically significant rise in blood pressure following the prayer session ($ps < .007$); however, patients also demonstrated a rise (systolic only) after exposure to the non-religious text ($p < .019$) (diastolic, $p = .876$).

Table 4
Vital Signs: Prayer and non-religious text conditions
Mean (SD)

	Before Prayer	After Prayer	Before Non-rel. Text	After Non-rel. Text
Body Temp.	98.24 (1.23)	98.34 (1.14)	98.26 (1.05)	98.24 (1.05)
Respiratory Rate	18.56 (1.74)	18.94 (1.13)	18.62 (1.28)	18.53 (1.41)

Table 4.1

Blood Pressure: Prayer and non-religious text conditions

	Before Prayer	After Prayer	Before Non-rel. Text	After Non-rel. Text
Blood Pressure	102.51 / 64.67	105.94 / 65.25	102.74 / 64.55	103.12 / 64.87

Across three dimensions, patients demonstrated statistically significant elevations in physiological function following participation in the prayer session. Findings suggest that participation in the prayer session was associated with physiological arousal. However, it is important to emphasize that although condition differences achieved statistical significance, alterations in body function were quite subtle and should not be considered clinically significant. Nevertheless, differences were in the expected direction and consistent with the contention that prayer impacts on the patients physical state (Al-Kandari, 2003, Helm, 2000, Koening et. al., 1998); albeit, pre- post-prayer differences subtle.

SUMMARY

In this chapter, the principal investigator presented the results of the surveys and vital sign recordings for the 60 participants. The findings can be summarized as follows:

1) Religiosity/spirituality scores were associated with level of spiritual strength, comfort and hope felt from prayers. They felt a greater degree of mental clarity after the prayer session, although it was not statistically significant.

2) In regards with vital signs, prayer has a positive relationship with physical health. The results of vital signs analysis showed that prayer is not clinically significant, but does have a statistically significant effect on patients.

The significance of these findings is discussed in the next chapter.

CHAPTER V

Discussion of Findings

DISCUSSION OF FINDINGS

INTRODUCTION

The purpose of this study was to investigate whether prayer has a positive effect on the well-being of Muslim patients. A review of the related literature supports the hypothesis that prayer has affected patients' well-being. The interpretation of quantitative data collected from the surveys and vital sign recordings during the present study is consistent with prior studies suggesting a beneficial impact on patients.

The result of this study suggests that prayer affects patients positively. It reduces stress and depression, gives comfort and hope, and alters blood pressure, respiratory rate, and body temperature. This study also draws attention to religion as holding a significant role in the lives of Muslim patients.

In the present study, patients completed three surveys: 1) pre-test survey; 2) religious reading post-test survey; and 3) non-religious reading post-test survey. Vital signs of sixty patients were also recorded and analyzed. The data reported in the previous chapter entitled Research Findings are analyzed and discussed under two sections: a) patients' response patterns on surveys, and b) physical effects of prayer on Muslim patients.

PATIENTS' RESPONSE PATTERNS ON SURVEYS

The analysis of the surveys reveals that higher scores on religiosity and spirituality are associated with lower depression and anxiety, and correlated negatively with measure of loneliness and despair. Moreover, positive relationships between self-reported religiosity and hopefulness and confidence were observed. A greater degree of religiosity is associated with hopefulness and confidence.

Numerous studies in US, some which include studies on Muslim patients, demonstrated that prayer does have an effect on patients. In a survey of 5,000 individuals, the investigators found that participants who prayed achieved good health, exhibited more favorable health-related behaviors and preventive service use, and reported greater satisfaction with care (O'Connor, Pronk, Tan, & Whitebird 2005, 369-75, and Puchalski 2001). Furthermore, 80% of published studies found religious commitment, including prayer, is related to better health outcomes (Mathews et al. 1998, 118). Religious commitment may help prevent many health problems, such as depression, substance abuse, and other illnesses (Levin & Vanderpool 1991, 9:41-64). Benson, Director Emeritus of the Mind-Body Medical Institute, in individual reporting found that those with strong religious beliefs were less likely to be depressed (1997, 173-174).

ANALYSIS OF PRELIMINARY SURVEY RESPONSE PATTERNS

A preliminary survey was used to determine the level of religiosity/ spirituality (from an Islamic perspective). The preliminary survey was also used to assess the intensity of depressive and anxiety symptoms as well as related variables reflecting the patient's emotional well-being (such as the degree of despair and loneliness).

The principal investigator compared the level of religiosity/spirituality with the scores on items assessing the intensity of depression, anxiety, loneliness, despair, hopefulness, and confidence. The influence of prayer on the patient's religiosity/spirituality and psychological well-being was investigated. The religiosity/spirituality score for the preliminary survey consisted of items assessing the degree or level of participation of submissiveness to the will of God (question 5), participation in religious activities per week (9), *salat*, five daily prayers (14), *zakat*, alms (21), *sadaqa*, charity (22), recitation of Qur'an (24), contemplation about death and the Hereafter (25).

Religiosity/Spirituality

On a range from 0-69, patients averaged a religiosity/spirituality score of 52.1. On a scale of 0-10 (0 representing an absence of the variable), patients rated themselves as having an average depression level of 2.01, an anxiety level of 2.81, a loneliness level of 1.81, a despair level of 1.91, a hopefulness level of 6.89 and a confidence level of 6.50.

The data show a negative correlation between religiosity/spirituality and psychological discomfort. There is a positive relationship between religiosity/spirituality and hopefulness/confidence. Findings are consistent with prior studies on prayer-health relationship. Patients displaying anxiety symptoms and described as religious who received religious-cultural psychotherapy in Malaysia showed more rapid improvement than those in the control group. Religious anxiety patients demonstrated greater symptoms in comparison to control patients (religious patients nor undergoing religious-cultural psychotherapy) (Razzali, Aminah, Khan 2002).

In this study, an overwhelming number of patients reported religiosity/spirituality scores of 75%, indicating that religion plays a great role in the participants' lives. Not every patient fulfills every obligation in religion; however, most fulfill some obligations. For example, a substantial number of respondents (76.6%) fast the full thirty days of Ramadan, while less than half (43.3%) perform the *salat*. The highest score of the seven questions for religiosity/spirituality was for *sadaqa*, where 95% of patients reported giving charity at least once a month, followed by a significant number of participants (93.3%) contemplated of death and the Hereafter on a weekly basis. More than half (65%) gave *zakat*, alms, read Qur'an weekly (63.3%), and participated in religious activities weekly (61.4%).

Islam affects many aspects of Muslim life. Therefore, most Muslims practice or participate in at least some religious and spiritual activity. The importance of religion in participants' lives is reflected by the fact that 71.6% rated religion as important. Some patients said that if they lived closer to a mosque or Islamic center, they would be able to participate in religious activities more often. In addition, they reported that their jobs sometimes conflict with their religious practices, such as attending the Friday congregational prayer.

The level of remembrance or God is also considerably high as Islamic practices involve invocation of God's name in almost any activity. A Muslim says *bismillah*, "In the Name of God" upon beginning any task, such as eating or working.

ANALYSIS OF RELIGIOUS POST-TEST SURVEY

Religiosity/spirituality scores were positively correlated with hopefulness and confidence and negatively correlated with depression, anxiety, loneliness, and despair. When a person performs prayer, makes *dhikr* or recites Qur'an, he or she concentrates his or her mind and bodily movements on the performance of the prayer, and redirects his/her focus away from worldly thoughts (Rahman 1987, 44). Benson's idea supports this practice as an effective way to ignore distressing thoughts and relax (as mentioned earlier in the Theoretical Considerations section).

According to the Qur'an and *hadith* (sayings of Prophet Muhammad, peace be upon him), prayer, including *salat*, *du'a*, *dhikr*, and Qur'anic recitation, brings a person closer to God (Qur'an 2:152, Riyadhus Saliheen, 883). This leads to a decrease in loneliness as a supplicant feels that he or she is being heard. Moreover, participants who perform *salat* also attend mosques, socialize within the Muslim community, and receive emotional and spiritual support. For example, it is a custom in most Muslim communities to announce in the mosque the hospitalizations and deaths of other Muslim in the area and ask for the congregation to pray and visit those Muslims.

Prayer also reminds a Muslim that God is all powerful and the Healer, so he or she should rely on God. In the religious post-test survey, significant number of patients (80%) affirmed their increased reliance on God after the prayer. The Qur'an orders believing Muslims to have hope and not despair at any time (3:139). Despair, cutting off hope from God's help and mercy, is even considered heresy (12:87). Muslims build spiritual strength results from faith and trust in God (Rahman 1987, 43). Prayers suppress anxiety and resentment or anger towards God (Rahman, 44). Contemplating about the life Hereafter, hoping for eternal happiness, all while relying on God's help and seeking medical treatment gives Muslims confidence in overcoming their illness, reduces their fear of death and suffering, and increases their ability to cope with hardships. All of these factors decrease anxiety, depression, and despair.

Comments made by patients participating in the present study, particularly those with life-threatening illnesses, reflect the findings of the study. One patient said, "Prayer gives me strength to struggle [with illness]." In general, patients felt comfort after prayers. "Whenever I feel stressed, I feel better after I make *du'a*." Patients' religious activities varied, though many perform some type of prayer, make *dhikr* or *du'a* on a daily basis. One says, "I always pray before I go to sleep." This illustrates the role of prayer in dealing with illness and stress. One patient even said that "without faith and prayer, I would commit suicide." This patient was diagnosed with lung cancer and told by doctors that he could live for possibly two more years. He told the principal investigator that whenever he prays, he offers supplication afterwards and cries. Afterwards, he feels great comfort and a sense of lightness, like the burden is relieved from his shoulders. Another patient spoke of how anxious he had felt before surgery, but made *du'a* and felt less anxious.

A COMPARISON OF RELIGIOUS AND NON-RELIGIOUS SURVEY DATA

The principal investigator administered a demographic and preliminary self-assessment survey before the prayers and a post-test survey was completed after the prayers. In the second session, a non-religious text was read to serve as a control to determine if the *du'as* were affecting the patient. The non-religious text was in Arabic, just like the *du'as* and invocations, but did not contain religious references. In the Findings section, the questions were divided into continuous data, where patients gave a rating from 1-10 (see Table 2), and dichotomous data, where patients responded with "yes" or "no" (see Table 3). The scores from the religious post-test surveys were separate from the non-religious post-test survey results. Due to the difference in data measurement, continuous data and dichotomous data is analyzed separately.

In the continuous data, religious text scores were higher than non-religious text scores. Patients reported a greater degree of comfort and spiritual strength following the prayer session. A substantial number of patients (83.3%) reported that they felt God's presence after the religious text in contrast with the non-religious text when 13.3% responded that they felt God's presence. According to Islamic theology, God is always present, so these participants understood the question from this point of view.

In the dichotomous data, the differences between religious and non-religious surveys were greater (see Table 3). The non-religious text was used as a control to find out whether the principal investigator's presence or the religious text was affecting the participants' responses. Even though participants were less interested in the non-religious text, some patients expressed their pleasure in the chaplain's presence.

Physical effects

Healing with prayer in Islamic tradition dates back to the Prophet Muhammad. The Prophet would pray for ill persons then recommend certain prayers and *du'as* for comfort. To a man who felt stomach pains, he said, "Arise and pray; for verily in prayer there is cure" (Al-Suyuti 1962, 157). Following this tradition, Muslim scholars throughout the centuries have maintained that healing involves physical, psychological, and spiritual processes. Al-Dhahabi wrote of how *salat*, ritual prayer, benefits both the body and soul (Rahman 1987, 44). Al-

Jawziyyah viewed *salat* as an exercise for the body and a comfort to the soul (1999, 109).

Modern studies endeavored to explore the physical effects of prayer from a scientific standpoint. Hundreds of studies have explored the relationship between health and religiosity and spirituality. Researchers at the Mayo Clinic reviewed 350 studies examining the influence of religion on physical health and 850 studies investigating the impact of religion on mental health supported contenting hypothesis that religion enhances illness prevention, coping with illnesses, and recovery (Mueller et. al. 2001, 76:1225-1235). In another study, investigators reported that 80% of published research works on prayer and healing write that religious commitment is associated with better health status and outcomes (Matthews et. al, 1998).

In terms of the Islamic prayers, Al-Tharshi strongly supported the idea that prayer improves physical well-being through exercise. By studying the different movements in ritual prayer, he concluded that *salat* is similar to light exercises in aiding the upkeep of the body (1992, 97-123).

The present study did not examine the physical effects of the *salat*, ritual prayer, in the session. Patients who performed *salat* were asked about how they felt after they performed *salat*. On an item assessing the degree of comfort following *salat*, patients obtained a mean score of 6.05 (on a range of 0-10) in the pre-test survey. On the degree of comfort after the test session, patients scored 5.10 out of 10 in the post-test survey.

The pre-test survey asked patients about the comfort they feel when they perform *salat* before admission while the post-test survey asked about the comfort they felt after the prayer session for the study. The discrepancy in these scores may be due to the different nature of worship of a non-hospitalized person compared to a hospitalized one. A Muslim performing *salat* recites the Qur'an, moves the body in various positions, and supplicates. A hospitalized patient does not have the ability to benefit from the physical movement of the *salat*. On the post-test surveys, when asked if they felt prayer affected their physical condition, 55% responded "Yes", 33.3% responded "No", and 11.6% were not sure or did not respond.

Patients gave different reasons as to why they felt prayer had a positive impact on their health. One patient pointed to the _wudu_, the ablution, before the prayer, as cleansing his body. Several patients noted that prayer reduces their stress, and one patient believed that prayer decreased his chances of stress-related illnesses. A middle-aged contractor reported that he finds prayer refreshing when he takes two or three breaks during his workday to perform _wudu_, ablution, and finds a quiet place to pray. One man stated that he has difficulty falling asleep and would read Qur'an to help him sleep in peace. An elderly Muslim appreciated that _salat_ exercised his body with light easy movements for a total of forty minutes a day.

Self-reports show that more than half of the study population held that prayer does have some positive effects on their physical conditions. Patients' views on the benefits of prayer reflect those of the studies mentioned in this section. Patients who pray on a regular basis find comfort in their daily lives as well.

Vital signs

Body temperature and respiratory rate

Based on the analysis of Dr. Burak Alptekin, there are no clinically significant changes in body temperature and respiratory rate before and after prayer and non-religious text (see Table 4). There are statistical changes, but those are also not significant enough to support the positive effects of prayer on physical well-being. These minor differences in pre-test and post-test conditions could have resulted from other factors, such as medication or intravenous therapy (IV). Dr. Alptekin mentioned that minor changes could result from possible fallibility of recordings. However, for the twelve patients who remained at the hospital for an extended period of time, post-test data show that prayer lowered their blood pressure.

Blood pressure

In the present study, the results of the analysis of vital signs support the positive relationships other researchers have found between prayer and blood pressure. In a related study on Islamic prayer and blood pressure, Al-Kandari tested 223 Kuwaitis blood pressure and compared the blood pressure of those who pray to those who do not. He concluded that those who pray were generally found with lower-blood pressure. Al-Kandari also documented the cultural and religious backgrounds of the participants and noted that involvement in religious activities seemed to be a factor in lowering blood pressure as it provided a social support network. Al-Kandari cites Byrne and Price (1979) who point out that two of the most important functions of religion for human health are providing sense of security and a source of strength from social support from the religious community. He suggests religiosity may be associated with a lower level of blood pressure because it improves one's ability to cope with stress and offers social support (2003, 12-13). Steffen (2003) also invoked as an explanatory hypothesis when his research results revealed that African Americans who engage in prayer and religious activities demonstrated lower blood pressure.

One other study looked at the movements of joints and muscles during *salat* and calculated blood pressure at different positions. Researchers found that during *salat*, movements increased cerebral blood flow and postural reflexes and helped the rehabilitation process of disabled geriatric patients by improving blood flow and increasing muscoskeletal fitness (Reza, Urakami & Mano, 2002).

In my research, I observed a significant change in the blood pressure of some critically-ill patients and patients who remain hospitalized for an extended period of time. Dr. Alptekin reported that a blood pressure change of 10mmHg (millimeter of mercury) is medically significant. Twelve of the long-term patients, 20% of participants, were recorded with changes between 5-10 mmHg. When factored into the average of all participants, these changes are not clinically meaningful. However, there is a need for further studies on the effects of prayer on patients who are critically ill and are hospitalized for an extended period of time.

While patients stated that prayer was associated with a relaxed state, modifications in vital signs of many participants were not consistent with that claim. Although there was little evidence of modification in physiological state, participants reported substantial changes in their physical/emotional and spiritual condition after prayer. Al-Kandari stated that congregational prayer and commitment to a religious group provides social support and improves stress management (2003, 468).

Furthermore, some limitations in terms of research may have affected outcomes. First, it should be noted that the hospital environment is not always the most suitable environment for prayer due to distractions by machine sounds and other people, such as staff, family members, and room-mates. A more ideal environment would be a quiet, more private and relaxing room. Second, vital signs were recorded for only *du'a*, verbal supplications, *dhikr*, invocation, and Qur'anic recitation, but not for *salat*, which theologically hold the most important role of all Islamic prayers. It was not possible to ask patients to perform the *salat* as it requires making ablution, special clothing, and bodily movements difficult for many patients. Also, special equipment would be required to measure the vital signs of praying patients. In their research, Reza, Urakami, and Mano (2002) reported that performing *salat* by geriatric patients was associated with positive outcomes, such as improving cerebral circulation and serving as a remedial action to depression. Further studies on *salat* and healing are necessary to understand the effects of *salat* on Muslim patients.

SUMMARY

In this chapter, the data were analyzed and discussed in two subsections: a) patients' response patterns on surveys; and b) physical effects of prayer on Muslim patients. The preliminary survey revealed that participants' level of religiosity/spirituality were already high as a result of the influence of Islamic practices on many aspects of Muslims' lives. Post-test surveys showed that prayer decreased anxiety, despair, depression, and loneliness through increased reliance on and hope in God.

Physiological data in the present study support previous studies, particularly those investigating the relationship between blood pressure and prayer. Other studies have pointed to the social support as a mediating factor in the positive relationship between prayer and health. The current study found statistically significant, yet clinically insignificant changes of physiological conditions. Unlike other studies, this study did not evaluate social support.

The present study supports the hypothesis that prayer does have positive effects on the patients based on participants' reports and recordings of vital signs. These effects are only immediate religious/ spiritual and physical effects. Also, the prayers used in this study do not include *salat* in the physical measurements.

To obtain more accurate results, each of the questions in the surveys deserves sole focus in research studies. There have been studies on only *salat*, *du'a*, intercessory prayer, and so on (refer to Literature Review). These studies give a more detailed picture of each Islamic practice. Long-term studies that use a larger participant group should provide more accurate data. Research can be carried out in different hospitals and hospices in the US and around the world. The findings may give us a better understanding of prayer's effect on Muslim patients who may practice religion differently. This research presents only a brief glimpse on the effects of these practices on well-being. A multi-disciplinary approach, in which involve psychologists, doctors, pastoral care staff work together in exploring this issue, may help us gain greater insight into the nature of the relationship between prayer and health.

Some Cases of Healing after Prayer

There are a substantial number of case reports describing individuals in the Muslim community who have been healed through prayer. The author has served as a Muslim chaplain for over twenty years in Turkey, Australia and the US and I have documented hundreds of cases of healing in response to prayer. Indeed, I have collected hundreds of narratives from Muslims of different ethnic backgrounds. Consider the following:

Boston, Massachusetts, USA

In 2006, a patient from an African country gave birth to a sickly child. Sadly, the patient died 11 days later. The newborn infant was placed on life support and spent two months in the intensive care unit. Moreover, the child had been diagnosed with a terminal illness.

The infant's doctors met several times to discuss the condition of the baby. Her physicians concluded that the infant was experiencing intense pain and had no chance of survival. As the Muslim chaplain at the hospital, I was asked by the infant's doctors to meet with the child's father and convince him that the best course of action was to remove the child from support and end her suffering. When I met with the father, he told me of his dying wife's wish for her daughter to be kept alive and her efforts to continue praying during her final days. His wife strongly believed that their daughter would survive, and told her husband that he should not agree to have the child removed from life-support. It was my understanding that the father would never agree with the doctors' recommendation to remove the infant from life support.

Not long after our conversation, the infant was transferred to another hospital. A year later, I contacted the father. He proudly informed me that his daughter was alive and living in California.

Boston, Massachusetts, USA

In 2005, MT underwent surgery on his hip; however, he continued to experience pain in the area that had been operated on. Over a two-year period, his physicians were unable to identify the cause of MT's pain despite numerous tests. They suggested that it may be psychological in origin; however, MT was not convinced. He consulted with different specialists at different hospitals as well.

Finally, he went to see an imam and described his pain symptoms. The imam recommended that he recite some of the supplications of the

Prophet Muhammad on a daily basis alongside his medical treatment. Within several weeks, MT reported that the pain had diminished.

Boston, Massachusetts, USA

In 2005, an Albanian man who was visiting his children in the US exhibited strange behavior and was hospitalized. The patient received a schizophrenia diagnosis. His son recalled that his exhibited similar signs while they were in Albania. At that time, his father was taken to an imam. He was not able to receive proper medical treatment due to lack of health insurance. The imam read parts of the Qur'an and offered supplications. Following his meeting with the imam, the man no longer demonstrated signs of psychiatric illness.

In Boston, the father underwent two weeks of inpatient treatment. Since the man had been exhibiting self-injurious behavior, staffers were forced to tie his hands to the bed. The son called for an imam and asked for spiritual healing methods to be applied on his father along with standard therapeutic intervention. The imam came a few times during the week. Within five days, the father was discharged and returned home to Albania.

Boston, Massachusetts, USA

In 2006, a boy in his teens was apparently experiencing disturbing visual hallucinations. His parents took him to the hospital where he underwent psychiatric therapy. Over the next few weeks, the boy failed to improve.

At that point, the young man's parents asked an imam to visit their son and pray for him. On a number of occasions, the imam came to the hospital and recited parts of the Qur'an including the first chapter of the Qur'an (Opening Chapter), the Verse of the Throne (*Ayat al-Kursi*), the last three chapters of the Qur'an, and some invocations (*dhikr*) of God's name. The imam also instructed the parents and the teenage boy to recite the verses daily. According to the mother, the boy appeared to improve and was discharged after ten days.

When the boy failed to follow the instructions of the imam after being discharged, he began to see strange things and exhibit odd behavior. Again, his parents took him to the hospital. They resumed the recitations and invocations given to them by the imam. The boy reported that he was feeling better and was discharged.

Brooklyn, New York, USA

In 1999, a pre-teen girl displayed strange movements at home and at school. She would stare at one point for a long period of time, twitch while sitting, and other unnatural tics. Her parents took her to the hospital where she was seen by doctors and psychologists. The child's parents also took her to see a Sufi master who prayed on her behalf. The Sufi master instructed the parents to read certain supplications twice a day. After two months, the girl no longer exhibited the peculiar behavior.

Pennsylvania, USA, 2007

This story was reported in *Vatan Gazetesi*, (December 2, 2007) a Turkish daily newspaper. In 2007, a doctor's newborn child had been born prematurely at six and a half months and was suffering from an illness. The infant required special machinery to breath properly. Moreover, physicians had warned the couple that the child would be born disabled.

Soon after the birth, the doctor visited Fethullah Gülen, a well-known Turkish Islamic scholar living in Pennsylvania at that time. The doctor mentioned his child's illness to Gülen, and Gülen wrote a prayer for the man to recite. Gülen also prayed for the child's health. The next day, the doctor left Gülen's home. He was on his way to the airport when he decided to call his wife. She happily informed him that their baby was breathing normally.

Southestern Turkey

I heard this case from the father of a patient. In 1964, a father living in a rural area in southeastern Turkey was worried about his four-year-old son who would lean against the wall and slowly shake his head left and right. This peculiar shaking of the head would last for almost ten minutes and would occur several times throughout the day.

At that time, it was not possible for rural people to seek psychological or psychiatric help, so they often turned to imams for spiritual healing. The local imam recited some verses from the Qur'an, offered a prayer, and instructed the father to recite certain prayers as well. The father followed the imam's instructions and reported that his boy soon stopped exhibiting the strange behavior.

Adiyaman, Turkey

Sheikh Muhammed Rasid, a Sufi master living in the village of Menzil, Adiyaman was known for his ability to help individuals overcome drug addiction. The Sufi master's reputation attracted substance abusers from many regions in Turkey. Thousands of individuals would visit the master in an attempt to end their dependence on alcohol or other drugs. Due to this, the Sufi lodge where the master resided was visited by thousands every month. I have met with individuals residing in many Turkish cities who had visited the Sufi master. They have shared their experiences with me.

The Sufi master first asked the substance user to shower (*ghusl*) to begin the process of outer purification, followed by sincere repentance (*tawbah*) for inner purification. Then the master gave the substance abuser specific spiritual tasks. He asked the substance abuser to invoke the name of God a minimum of 1000 times daily (*dhikr*) and to perform the five daily prayers. During their visit, substance abusers established relations with members of the Sufi order residing in their home town or city. Thus, the former substance abuser gradually establishes a new social network, which in turn, eventually modifies their lifestyle.

Since the Sufi master does not maintain records, it is difficult to determine, precisely, how many substance abusers have successfully recovered; however, I can attest to the fact that many individuals succeeded in breaking free of their addiction. In fact, I encountered several individuals who had benefited from the Sufi master's procedure in every city. I visited during my travels across Turkey over the 25 years.

I questioned these individuals to further understand how the rehabilitation process worked. I noted several common features. First, they had all been abusing substances for some time and their addictive behaviors had caused major problems at work and within in the family. Second, they had clearly intended to overcome the addiction and had been actively seeking solutions. Third, they pledged allegiance to the Sufi order, hence entering into a social circle that would support them through their rehabilitation and provide them with a new social life devoid of most worldly temptations.

I also met with those who did not follow all of the Sufi master's instructions. They failed to overcome the addiction or experienced periods of abstinence followed by relapse. Indeed, only those who followed the tasks and continued the religious practices described above succeeded in overcoming the addiction. The credit may not go to the Sufi master alone. One must factor in the character and the determination of the individual, the substance used, additional sources of social support (e.g., the family), and religious acts.

Istanbul, Turkey

In 2009, I met with AB, a businessman who owns several factories. One day, his neck got locked in a certain position. He could not move his neck and experienced pain. He sought medical assistance and followed the medical advice he received. Over the next two months, he received physical therapy and medication.

One day, he visited a terminally ill patient in the hospital where he underwent physical therapy. The terminal patient was known to be a pious man who was a devoted Muslim and had been active in the community. The patient saw AB's condition and recited verses from the Qur'an and offered a prayer. While reciting, the patient rubbed AB's neck. He finished by saying, "By the grace of God, you will get better." AB walked out of the hospital. After a few minutes, he was surprised that he could move his neck. By the time he arrived at home, he could move his neck normally. He did not feel the need for further medical treatment.

Sydney, New South Wales, Australia

In 1995, FR was diagnosed with cancer and was told that she would die within 3 to 6 months. FR refused to accept this "death sentence" and stated that she must continue to care for her young children. While weeping, she prayed to God for a recovery. She lived for another ten years and died soon after all her children had married.

North Sydney, New South Wales, Australia

In 1996, an Indian Christian woman living in North Sydney was worried when her husband began complaining that someone was controlling him, sapping his energy, causing him to faint, and making him see strange things. After a long period of testing and ineffective treatment, he underwent brain surgery; however, he continued to experience distressing neuropsychiatric symptoms. The woman's mother was a Muslim living in South Africa. She suggested that her daughter ask an imam to pray for the husband. Desperate for help, she asked an imam at the Gallipoli Mosque in Auburn, NSW, to pray for her husband's recovery. The imam visited their home over a period of three weeks and recited passages from the Qur'an, and prayed for the husband. After three weeks, her husband reported that some of the strange phenomena (e.g., shaking furniture, odd smells, and unfamiliar voices and sounds) had stopped occurring. It wasn't a full recovery; however, many of his disturbing symptoms had disappeared, and it was a relief from the psychologically disturbing symptoms.

Dandenong, Victoria, Australia

In 2002, EM had an illness when she was a child, and became paralyzed as a result. Over the years, her parents took her to various doctors. Nothing would reverse the paralysis. Furthermore, she was unable to walk or talk, and was totally dependent on others. The doctors saw no hope in the girl walking again.

When EM was 16, her mother had a dream during which she heard a voice. The voice instructed her to take her daughter to Turkey to Eyub al-Ansari's tomb near the Eyub Sultan Mosque in Istanbul and pray to God for her daughter's recovery out of His love for this Companion of the Prophet who hosted Prophet Muhammad when he had to immigrate to Madinah. Eyub al-Ansari later died in Istanbul during an conquest attempt.

The woman took her daughter to the mosque in a wheelchair and prayed as instructed. Within a few weeks, the girl slowly began to show the ability to move and talk. When they returned to Australia from Turkey, the girl did not need a wheelchair. She was walking on her own and her speech was a bit slurred, but could be understood.

Broadmeadows, Victoria, Australia

In 2001, AK's wife was pregnant with their first child. After several tests, the doctors told the couple that the male fetus had a hole in his heart and the infant would either die during the birth process or be born handicapped. The physicians suggested that the couple terminate the pregnancy. The couple thought it over, but could not accept abortion. They both cried and pleaded with God to grant them a healthy child. At their next check-up, their doctor examined an X-ray and reported that the hole was no longer present. The doctor was shocked and said, "It's a miracle." The child is alive and doing well.

Indianapolis, IN, USA

Dr. Shahin Athar, Clinical Professor of Medicine at Indiana University School of Medicine presented the following case history on March 7, 1997 at the 4th Annual Convention of International Association for Sufism (IAS) in San Francisco, California. Dr. Athar is also the Chairman of the Medical Ethics of Islamic Medical Association of North America and a Member of the IAS. He is the author of "Health Concerns for Believers" and has edited a book entitled "Islamic Perspective in Medicine." Dr. Athar described the following case history: He visited a critically ill patient who had an adrenal tumor (pheochromocytoma) and was in hypotensive shock. He asked her what could he do for her and she, out of desperation (doctors had told her she she would soon die) asked him to pray. So he placed his hand over the site of the tumor and recited the Prophetic prayer. The next day, he was surprised to see her sitting up in bed and smiling. She told him that the radiologist had scanned her again and found no trace of the tumor. He could not explain it but thought that the arteriogram may have "infracted the tumor."

Uzbekistan

In 1991, Johan Rasanayagam, a medical researcher, conducted field studies in the central Asian nation of Uzbekistan. In an article describing his studies, he provided several examples of those who recovered through spiritual means.

He encountered an epileptic man who was healed through dreaming: When he was ill (epilepsy) and in the hospital, he performed the evening prayers, went to sleep, and had a dream in which he saw a house that he had never visited before. When he sought it out, it turned out to be the house of a *bakshi* (spiritual healer)... He continued to go to the *bakshi* for his own healing [in the dream]. He described a healing experience. He was visited by the *bakshi*'s spirit helpers, a black man and woman, who read the Qur'an over him. They were followed by a doctor and a nurse in white gowns who did an operation on his side, where he had been experiencing some pain. When he woke up later, he felt fine and his epilepsy was cured (2006, 393).

There are still more than a hundred incidents that I have not recorded in this book that I have either directly witnessed or documented after discussing the events with a patient or a patient's relative. If an academic research study was conducted to determine the numbers of those healed with prayer, it could not be compared to the number of those individuals who prayed but were not healed. However, people do not commit the latter to memory or emphasize them as much as the miraculous outcomes. As Nursi observed, the aim of prayer is not to see its benefit in this world with the granting of what is desired, but to fulfill the duty of praying and expect the reward in the Hereafter. To pray only for worldly benefit contradicts the criteria of prayer, and would not witness any benefit in this world (Nursi, 1996, 196).

Chapter VI

Conclusion

CONCLUSION

Contemporary research and empirical studies in the West and Muslim world point to the benefits of praying during illness. Praying during sickness produces physical benefits like reduced blood-pressure (Al-Kandari 2003), psychological/emotional benefits such as a decrease in depression and fear, and spiritual benefits such as preparation for death.

The present study supports previous works with similar findings. Prayer holds an important role in the life and recovery process of the Muslim patients who were surveyed. Many stated that prayer became more important for them during their illness. Patients listed prayer as giving them comfort and believed that prayer had a positive effect on their recovery.

In the current study, the analysis by a team of professionals supports the hypothesis of the positive effect of prayer on the well-being of Muslim patients. Burak Alptekin, MD., concluded that prayer lowers blood-pressure, especially for patients with more serious and terminal diseases and requires extended hospitalization. Wayne Dinn, a neuropsychological researcher, assisted with the data analysis, which revealed that prayer was associated with higher scores on self-report measure of patients. Imam Talal Eid, Th.D., and the principal investigator found that prayer increases the religiosity and spirituality of Muslims during illness. The principal investigator observed during the test sessions that patients appear to be more relaxed after participating in the prayer session.

Based on the results of this research, other studies, and my personal experience as a chaplain, Muslim clergy should play a greater role in the healing process. Hospital staff in the West may have little or no knowledge of the needs of Muslim patients in terms of religion, spirituality, and culture. A Muslim chaplain can train hospital staff in these matters and provide for the Muslim patients, especially for Muslims who are not well educated or have little knowledge in matters of religion and thus may not know how to pray, read the Qur'an, and understand or know about the Hereafter. They may face greater psychological and emotional distress in the face of illness and possible death, and high levels of anxiety may worsen their physical condition. As described in the Literature Review, Islamic practices, including prayer, prepare a Muslim for the difficulties of sickness and death in three ways:

1) When healthy, a Muslim takes physical preventative measures against illness such as following the hygiene traditions of the Prophet Muhammad. Through Islamic practices, he or she maintains a healthy attitude and develops a positive way of thinking towards sickness and other difficulties through relying on God's power, mercy, which in turn decreases their fears and gives them hope.

2) When ill, a Muslim will seek medical treatment as a religious duty. A Muslim will think positively about illness instead of feeling guilty or fearful. Praying during illness will aid the healing process through physical and spiritual comfort, and increase his or her hope.

3) Islamic practices and prayer prepares Muslims psychologically and spiritually for death by contemplating about death and the afterlife, praying to God for a peaceful death and eternal happiness. Thus, when facing a fatal illness, a Muslim belief in God's mercy and the Hereafter will comfort him or her by decreasing fear of nonexistence.

This research has added to thousands of prayer and health studies. This study, in particular, explored the effects of prayer in regards to the well-being of Muslim patients, and found many benefits. Alongside modern medicine, prayer can help improve health. Neglecting the spiritual and religious needs of the Muslim patients may not aid the healing process, and might even delay the process. It is sincerely hoped that this research will contribute to a greater understanding of the role of prayer in Muslim patients' well-being, and encourage non-Muslims, especially medical staff and other caretakers of Muslim patients to consider the healing power of prayer.

25 REMEDIES FOR THE SICK

By Bediüzzaman Said Nursi

NOTE: This treatise is taken from The Gleams, the Twenty-fifth Gleam, translated by Hüseyin Akarsu, The Light, Inc., 2008

This treatise was written as a medicine, a solace, a spiritual prescription, and as a visit wishing recovery for those who are ill.

A reminder and an apology

This spiritual prescription, which was written at great speed, has not been revised and has been left as it occurred to my heart. Therefore, I request the readers, and particularly the unwell, not to feel offended by any disagreeable expressions that may be contained within. I also request them to pray for me.

> Those who, when a disaster befalls them, say, "Surely we belong to God (as His creatures and servants), and surely to Him we are bound to return." (2: 156)

> "And He it is Who gives me food and drink; And Who, when I fall ill, heals me." (26: 79–80)

In this Gleam, we explain the twenty-five remedies which may offer true consolation for those who are ill or struck by misfortune, who make up one tenth of humankind.

The first remedy

You who are unhappy in your sickness! Do not be anxious, persevere instead. Your illness is not a loss for you, but a gain, a sort of cure. For life departs like capital. If it yields no fruits, it is wasted. And if it passes in ease and heedlessness, it is short, bringing almost no profit.

Illness makes that capital of yours yield huge profits. Moreover, it prevents your life from being short; it holds it back, lengthening or expanding it, so that it may depart after yielding its fruits. Indicating the fact that life lengthens through illness, this proverb is much renowned and widely circulated: "The time of disaster is very long; the time of enjoyment, very short."

The second remedy

You who are ill and lacking in perseverance! Do indeed persevere and offer thanks. Your illness may transform each of the minutes of your life that pass in illness into one hour's worship. For worship is of two sorts. One is that which is performed, the other is the sort which is not actually performed, but is suffered and thus leads to sincere supplication. Illnesses and disasters are examples of this sort. By means of these, those afflicted deeply feel their innate impotence and weakness; they take refuge in their All-Compassionate Creator and entreat, thus being able to perform sincere worship. There are authenticated narrations from God's noble Messenger, upon him be peace and blessings, that the times of believers which pass in illness are counted as worship, provided they do not complain about God.[1] It is also reliably narrated from the Messenger and there are reports from saints of spiritual discovery that one minute's illness of some patients who show perseverance with thankfulness equals one hour's worship, and a minute's illness of certain spiritually perfected individuals, equals the worship of a day. Therefore, rather than complaining, be thankful for the illness, which makes one minute of your life the equivalent of a thousand minutes and gains for you a long life.

The third remedy

You who are impatient in your illness! The fact that all those who come to this world inevitably depart, that the young grow old, and

---

[1]   *al-Bukhari*, "Jihad" 134; Ahmad ibn Hanbal, *al-Musnad*, 4:410. (Tr.)

that the world is perpetually turning amidst death and separation, testifies that humankind has not come to this world for enjoyment or pleasure. In addition, although humankind is the most perfect of living beings, the richest of beings in the equipment of life, and can virtually be regarded as their king, because of dwelling on past pleasures and worrying about future troubles, human beings lead a grievous, troublesome life, much lower than the animals. This shows that humankind has not come to this world to live in ease and pleasure. Rather, possessing vast capital, it has come here to work for an eternal life by doing the required trade. The capital given to it is its lifetime.

Were it not for illness, good health and ease would cause heedlessness, presenting the world as pleasant and making people oblivious of the Hereafter. By distracting them from the thought of death and the grave, good health and ease cause them to waste the capital of life on trifles. But illness suddenly gives them awareness, and says to the body: "You are not immortal, and have not been left to your own devices. You have a duty. Give up haughtiness; think of the One Who has created you; know that you will enter the grave, and make the necessary preparation!" Thus, from this perspective, illness is an advisor that never deceives; and it is an admonishing guide. For this reason, rather than complaining about illness, we should be thankful for it. If it gives much trouble and pain, we should show patience.

The fourth remedy

You who are ill and complaining! It is better for you not to complain, but to give thanks and show patience. For your body, with all its members and your faculties, is not your property. You have not made them, nor have you bought any of your bodily components from any workshop. They are the property of someone else. Their Owner has disposal over His property as He wills.

As stated in The Twenty-Sixth Word (included in *The Words*), a very rich and infinitely skilled clothes designer uses an ordinary man as a model to display his works of art and invaluable wealth in return for wages. For a brief hour, he clothes the model in a jeweled and artistically fashioned garment that he has made. He continues to modify the garment while the model wears it. In order to display his wonderful varieties of art, he cuts the garment, alters it, lengthening it here and shortening it there. Does the model employed for a wage have any right to say, "Your orders to bow and stand up are causing me trouble. Your cutting and shortening of this garment, which must make me more beautiful, spoils my beauty." Can the model accuse the designer of treating him unkindly and unfairly?

You who are ill! As in that simile, the All-Majestic Maker—in order to display the embroideries of His All-Beautiful Names and indeed make you more and more "beautiful"—causes you to undergo numerous, different states and situations in the garment of your body in which He has clothed you, bejeweled as it is with luminous faculties like seeing, hearing, reasoning, and feeling. Just as, through hunger, you learn of His Name, The All-Providing, so too through your illness, you come to know His Name, The All-Healing. Since suffering and disasters manifest the decrees and operations of some of His Names, there are in them gleams of wisdom, and rays of mercy, within which are numerous beauties. If the veil between us and His decrees and acts were to be lifted, you would find many agreeable and beautiful meanings behind the veil of illness, which you are frightened of and dislike.

The fifth remedy

You who are afflicted with illness! I have become convinced through experience at this time that illness is a Divine favor for some people, a gift of mercy. Although I am not worthy of it, for these last eight or nine years, a number of young people have visited me to pray for them because of their illnesses. I have noticed that compared to those of the same age, any unwell young person I have met has begun to think of the Hereafter. They are no longer in the typical intoxication of youth, and have saved themselves to a degree from the animal desires that are embedded in heedlessness. Based on this observation, I would remind them that their bearable illnesses are a Divine favor. I would say,

"Brother, I am not opposed to this illness of yours. I do not feel compassion for you due to your illness, so that I should pray for you. Try to show good patience until illness awakens you completely, and after it has completed its duty, God willing, the All-Compassionate Creator will cure you."

I would also say to them as follows:

> Because of the calamity of good health, some of your equals in age become heedless, and do not perform the five daily Prayers; they do not think of the grave, forget God, and damage, even destroy, the eternal life for the sake of the superficial pleasure of an hour's worldly life. But with the eye of illness, you see your grave, which you will in any case enter, and the mansions of the Hereafter beyond it, and act accordingly. This means that illness is good health for you, while the good health of some of your peers is in fact an illness for them.

The sixth remedy

You who are sick and complain of your suffering, I say to you: Think of your past life and remember the pleasurable, happy days and the distressing, troubled times. For sure, you will either say, "Oh!" or, "Ah!" That is, your heart and tongue will either say, "All praise and thanks be to God!" or, "Alas, alas!"

Notice that what makes you utter a sigh of relief and say, "All praise and thanks be to God!" is that your thinking of the sufferings and calamities that befell you in the past stirs up a kind of spiritual pleasure and causes your heart to be thankful. For the disappearance of suffering is a pleasure. The passing of sufferings and calamities left a lasting pleasure in the spirit. When it is stirred up through thinking, a pleasure pours forth from the spirit with thanks.

What makes you exclaim, "Alas, alas!" is the pleasurable and happy times you enjoyed in the past. Through cessation, they have left an unending pain in your spirit so that whenever you think of them, that pain is aroused and causes sorrow and regret to pour forth.

Since one day's illicit pleasure sometimes causes a year's spiritual suffering, while the pain of one day's temporary illness brings the pleasure of many days' rewards together with the pleasure of its cessation, think of the result of this temporary illness you are suffering now and the rewards it potentially bears. Say, "This too will pass, God willing!" and, instead of complaining, offer thanks.

Another sixth remedy

You, brother or sister in faith, who think of the pleasures of this world and are distressed by illness! If this world were eternal, and if on our way to eternity there were no death, and if the winds of separation and death did not blow, and if there were no "winters" of the spirit in the calamitous and stormy future, I would have pitied you along with you. But since the world will one day say to us, "Now, it is the time of departure!" and close its ears to our cries, warned by these illness, we must give up our love of it before it drives us out. Before it abandons us, we must try to abandon it in our hearts.

Illness reminds us of this reality and says, "Your body is not composed of stone and iron; rather it has been composed of various materials that are subject to partition and dissolution. Give up conceit, be aware of your innate impotence, recognize your Master, know your duties, and learn why you came to the world!" Illness says this secretly in the ear of the heart.

Also, since the pleasure and enjoyment of this world do not last and, particularly if they are licit, this is distressing and painful, do not weep over their disappearance because of illness. On the contrary, think of the worship you are performing by enduring the illness and the rewards that pertain to the Hereafter, and try to be content.

The seventh remedy

You who are ill and have lost the pleasures of health! Your illness does not ruin the contentment of the Divine blessing in health; rather, it causes you to taste it more deeply, and increases it. For if something continues uninterruptedly, it loses its effect. The people of truth agree that "things are known through their opposites." For example, were it not for darkness, light would not be known and it would give no pleasure. Without cold, heat would not be recognized, and would remain unpleasant. If there were no hunger, food would offer no delight. If there were no thirst, drinking water would give no satisfaction. Without illness, health and appetite would be without pleasure.

By endowing humans with numerous senses, organs, and faculties that they may taste and recognize the uncountable varieties of His bounties in the universe, the All-Wise Originator shows that He wills that humans may experience all the varieties of His bounties and give continual thanks. Therefore, as He grants good health and appetite, He will certainly give illnesses and pains. I ask you: If you were not suffering this discomfort in your head or hands or stomach, would you be mindful of the pleasure of the Divine favor of the good health in your head or hands or stomach, and offer thanks? Certainly, not only would you not have offered thanks, you would not have even considered it! You would have expended that good health unconsciously and heedlessly, and perhaps even wantonly.

The eighth remedy

You who are sick and now reflecting on the Hereafter! Like soap, sickness washes away the dirt of sins and cleanses. It is established in an authenticated *hadith* that illnesses are expiation for sins. It says, "As ripe fruits fall from the tree when it is shaken, so the sins of a believer fall away with the shaking during illness."[2]

Sins are perpetual illnesses in the eternal life. They are also illnesses for the heart, conscience, and spirit in this worldly life. If you persevere and do not complain, you are being saved from numerous perpetual illnesses through that temporary illness. But if you do not worry about sins, or are not aware of the afterlife, or do not recognize God, you have such an illness that it is a million times worse than your

---

[2] *al-Bukhari*, "Marda'" 1, 2, 13; *Muslim*, "Birr" 14. (Tr.)

present illness. Cry out at it, for your heart, spirit, and soul have relations with all the beings in the world. Your connections with them are
continually severed through decay, death, and separation, causing
innumerable wounds to open up in you. Particularly since you are not
aware of the Hereafter and imagine death to be eternal extinction, it is
as if you had a body afflicted with uncountable wounds and illnesses.
Therefore, what you must do first is to search for belief as the cure for
these innumerable spiritual wounds and illnesses of the ailing body.
You must correct your creed, and the shortest, most direct way to such
a cure is to recognize the Power and Mercy of an All-Powerful One of
Majesty through the window of your innate impotence and weakness,
which your physical illness shows you beneath the veil of heedlessness
that it has rent.

Indeed, one who does not recognize God is afflicted with a world-
ful of tribulations, while the world of one who recognizes God is full
of light and spiritual joy. Everyone is aware of this according to the
strength of their belief. The pain of physical illnesses melts away under
the spiritual joy, healing, and pleasure that come from belief.

The ninth remedy

You who are ill and acknowledge your Creator! People fear and are
distressed by illness because it sometimes leads to death. Since death is
frightening to the superficial, heedless view, illnesses that may lead to
it cause fear and worry.

So, first of all, know and believe with certainty that the appointed
hour of death is certain and does not change. It has many times
occurred that the healthy ones weeping beside the seriously ill have
died, while the seriously ill have been cured and continue to live.

Secondly, death is not frightening; it is not as it appears to be.
Based on the light provided by the wise Qur'an, we have convincingly
explained in many parts of the *Risale-i Nur* that for people of belief,
death is a discharge from the hardship of the duties of this life. It is also
a respite from worship, which is a drill and training in the arena of

trials in this world. Moreover, it is a means of reunion with ninety-nine relatives and beloved ones who have already emigrated to the other world. It is also a means of entering the true homeland and eternal abode of happiness. In addition, it is an invitation from the prison of the world to the spacious gardens of Paradise. And it is the time when one receives a wage from the grace of the All-Compassionate Creator in return for a service. Since this is the reality of death, we should view death not as something terrifying, but as the prelude to mercy and happiness.

Moreover, for some of the people of God, the fear of death is not terror of death itself, but rather on account of their hope, through the continuation of the duties of life, that they will gain more merit by performing more good works.

For the people of belief, death is the door to Divine mercy, while for the people of misguidance it is the pit of eternal darkness.

The tenth remedy

You who are ill and worrying needlessly! Your worry is because of the severity of your illness, but your worries make your illness more severe. If you want your illness to be less severe, try not to worry about it. That is, think about the benefits of your illness, the spiritual rewards it brings, and that it will pass quickly. Give up worrying, and cut off the illness at the root.

Indeed, worry doubles the burden of illness; in addition to your physical illness, it causes an immaterial illness in your heart, upon which the physical illness depends and through which it persists. If that worry vanishes through submission, resignation, and thinking of the wisdom inherent in the illness, one of the important roots of the illness will be severed. It becomes less severe and in part disappears. Sometimes a minor physical illness becomes tenfold just through worries and apprehension. When worries and apprehension cease, nine tenths of the illness disappears. In addition to increasing an illness, since worry is an accusation against Divine wisdom, a criticism of Divine Mercy, and a complaint about the All-Compassionate Creator, it causes counter-suffering, and increases illness.

Indeed, just as thankfulness increases favor, so too do complaints increase illnesses and suffering. Furthermore, worry is itself an illness. The cure for it is knowing the wisdom inherent in illness. Since you are now aware of the wisdom in illness and its benefits, apply that ointment to the worry and be relieved. Say, "Oh!" instead of, "Ah!" and "All praise be to God for every state!" instead of, "Alas!" and "Oh dear!"

The eleventh remedy

You, brother or sister in faith! You who are sick and impatient! Although your present illness causes you some suffering, all your former illnesses have produced an immaterial contentment for your spirit resulting in your recovery from them, and a spiritual pleasure arising from the reward received for enduring them. There may be no more illnesses from today on, even from this hour, so no pain can come from something that does not exist. And if there is no pain, there is no grief. But since you imagine otherwise, you are showing impatience. For all the times of illness before today have disappeared together with the pains they have caused, leaving the rewards the illness has brought and the pleasure their departure gives. So, when they should give you the feeling of profit and happiness, it is crazy to think of them and feel grieved, or to be impatient. The future days have not come yet. Thinking of them now and feeling grieved and showing impatience with thoughts about a day that does not exist, or an illness that does not exist, or a suffering that does not exist, and thus giving the color of existence to three degrees of non-existence—if that is not crazy, what is?

Since the times of illness before now have given happiness, and since the times subsequent to it and the illnesses and sufferings (you imagine they may bring) are non-existent, do not scatter the power of the patience God Almighty has given you to the right and left, but mobilize it against the pain of the present hour. Say, "O All-Patient One!" and endure it.

The twelfth remedy

You who on account of illness cannot perform your regular worship or invocations, and regret this! Know that it is stated in a *hadith*, "A pious, God-revering believer who, due to illness, cannot do the invocations he does normally and regularly, receives an equal reward."[3] Illness substitutes for the supererogatory Prayers of the ill person who does their obligatory worship as much as possible and shows patience in submissive reliance on God.

Furthermore, illness reminds people of their innate impotence and weakness, and causes them to pray both verbally and through the tongue of their state. God Almighty has created human beings with boundless impotence and weakness so that they continually seek refuge in the Divine Court and pray and supplicate. Since, according to the verse, *Say: "My Lord would not care for you were it not for your prayer,"* (25:77) the wisdom in the creation of humanity and the reason for its value are sincere prayer, and as illness leads people to such prayers, rather than complaining about illness, we should thank God, and should not turn off the fountain of prayer that has been caused to flow by illnesses.

The thirteenth remedy

You who are unhappy and complain of your illness! Illness is an important treasure and a very valuable Divine gift for some people. Every ill person can consider their illness from this perspective.

Our appointed hour of death is unknown to us. So, in order to save people from absolute despair and heedlessness and to keep them between fear and hope and in a position from which they may lose neither in the world nor in the Hereafter, God Almighty has concealed the appointed hour of death. Since death can come at any time, if it captures the human being in heedlessness, it may cause great harm to their eternal life. But illness dispels heedlessness, makes people think of

---

[3]   *Abu Dawud*, "Jana'iz" 1; Ahmad ibn Hanbal, *al-Musnad*, 4:418.

their afterlife and reminds them of death and thus prepares them for the Hereafter. They sometimes make such great profit that in twenty days they can gain a rank that they could not otherwise have gained in twenty years.

For instance, from among my friends there were two youths, may God have mercy on them, Sabri from the village of Ilema, and Vezirzade Mustafa from Islamköy. I used to note with amazement that although these two were illiterate and could not serve by copying the *Risale-i Nur*, they were among the foremost in sincerity and the service of belief. I did not know why that was so. After their deaths I understood that both had suffered from a serious illness. Guided by that illness, unlike other heedless youths who did not carry out the obligatory worship, they had great reverence for God, and performed the most valuable services, attaining a state beneficial to the Hereafter. God willing, the trouble of two years' illness was the means to the bliss of millions of years of eternal life. I now understand that the prayers I sometimes offered for their health were maledictions in respect to this world. I hope that my prayers were accepted for their well-being in the Hereafter.

Thus, it is my belief that these two gained a profit equal to that which can be gained through ten years' piety and righteousness (*taqwa*). If, like some young people, they had trusted in their youth and good health and let themselves fall into heedlessness and dissipation, and if death, which is always on the watch, had grasped them right in the midst of the filth of their sins, their graves would have been the lairs of scorpions and snakes, instead of that treasury of lights.

Since there are such benefits in illness, we should not complain about it, but bear it with patient reliance on God, indeed, with gratitude to Him and confidence in His Mercy.

The fourteenth remedy

You who are sick in that your eyes are afflicted with cataracts! If you knew what a light and spiritual seeing there is beneath the cataracts that may cover a believer's eyes, you would exclaim, "A hundred thousand thanks to my All-Compassionate Lord." I will relate an incident to you to explain this ointment. It is as follows:

One time, the aunt of Süleyman from Barla, who served me for eight years with perfect loyalty and without causing any resentment, became blind. Thinking well of me a hundred times more than was my due, that righteous woman caught me by the door of the mosque and asked me to pray for the recovery of her eyes. I therefore made that blessed woman's righteousness the intercessor for my prayer, and entreated, "O Lord! Restore her sight due to her righteousness." Two days later, an eye specialist from Burdur came and removed the cataracts. But forty days later she again lost her sight. I was much grieved and prayed for her earnestly. I hope that the prayer was accepted for her afterlife, or else my prayer was the most mistaken malediction for her. For there remained only another forty days until her death; forty days later she died—May God have mercy on her.

Thus, rather than looking sorrowfully at the pathetic gardens of Barla with the eye of old age, she profited by being able to gaze on the gardens of Paradise from her grave for forty thousand days, for she had a firm belief and was earnestly righteous.

If a believer loses their sight and enters the grave blind, they may, in accordance with their degree, gaze on the world of light to a much greater extent than the other people of the grave. Just as in this world we see many things that blind believers do not see, if they go from this world with belief, they see to a greater extent than the other people of the grave. As if looking through the most powerful telescopes, they can, in accordance with their degree, see and gaze on the gardens of Paradise as on a movie screen.

Thus, through thanks and patience you can find under the veil that exists on your present eye an eye that is light-filled and light-diffusing and with which you can see and gaze on Paradise above the heavens while under the soil. The eye specialist which will remove the veil from your present eye and enable you to look with that eye is the wise Qur'an.

The fifteenth remedy

You who are sick and sighing and lamenting! Do not consider the outward aspect of illness and sigh; consider its meaning and be content. If the meaning of illness was not good, the All-Compassionate Creator would not have given illness to His most-beloved servants. A *hadith* says, "Those afflicted with the severest trials are the Prophets, then those resembling them, and then those resembling the latter."[4] That is, those most afflicted with suffering and hardship are the best of people, the most perfect of them. The Prophets, including in particular the Prophet Job, upon him be peace, then the saints, and then those foremost in righteousness after the Prophets and saints have regarded the illnesses they have suffered as sincere worship and gifts from the All-Merciful. They have offered thanks in patience. They have seen these illnesses as surgical operations performed by the compassion of the All-Compassionate Creator.

O you who cry out and lament! If you want to join this light-diffusing caravan, offer thanks in patience. For if you complain, they will not admit you among them. You will fall into the pits of the people of misguidance, and go along a dark road.

Indeed, there are some illnesses which, if they lead to death, are like a sort of martyrdom. They cause one to gain some certain degree of sainthood. For example, like the believing women who die during or because of childbirth,[5] those who die from pains in the abdomen, and by drowning, burning, or the plague, are considered as martyrs.[6] There are also other such blessed illnesses which help to gain a degree of sainthood for those who die from them. Furthermore, since illness lessens the love of the world and attachment to it, it lightens the pain of parting from the world, which is extremely grievous for worldly people. Sometimes it makes such a departure desirable.

---

[4]   *at-Tirmidhi*, "Zuhd" 57; *Ibn Maja*, "Fitan" 23. (Tr.)

[5]   A child-bearing woman may gain some sort of martyrdom if she dies within forty days after giving birth.

[6]   *al-Buhari*, "Jihad" 30; *Muslim*, "'Imara" 164. (Tr.)

The sixteenth remedy

You who are sick and complain of your distress! Illness induces respect and compassion, which are most important and good for human social life. This saves people from conceited feelings of self-sufficiency, which drives them to unfriendliness and unkindness. For according to the reality stated in, *No indeed, but the human is unruly and rebels, in that he sees himself as self-sufficient* (96: 6–7), a carnal, evil-commanding soul which feels self-sufficient due to good health and well-being does not regard the many causes which are deserving of brotherhood. And they do not feel compassion towards the misfortune-stricken or ill, who should be shown kindness and pity. Yet, whenever they become ill, they are aware of their own innate impotence and neediness, and feel respect towards their sisters and brothers who are worthy of it. They pay respect to their believing brothers and sisters who visit or help them. And they feel human kindness, which originates in fellow-feeling and compassion for the disaster-stricken—a most important Islamic characteristic. Comparing others to themselves, they empathize with them, feel affection for them, and do whatever they can to help them. At the very least they pray for others and pay them a visit of consolation, which is a *Sunna* act according to the Shari'a,[7] thus earning reward.

The seventeenth remedy

You who are sick and complain of not being able to do good works due to illness! Offer thanks! It is illness that opens to you the door of the most sincere of good works. Illness is a most important means of continuously gaining reward for the sick person and for those who are looking after them for the sake of God; it is, in addition, a means for supplications to be accepted.

Certainly, there is significant reward for believers who look after the sick. Asking after the health of those who are ill and visiting them—provided it does not tax them—is a *sunna* act, an act highly

---

7   *Muslim,* "Birr" 40; *Abu Dawud,* "Jana'iz" 7; *at-Tirmidhi,* "Jana'iz" 2. (Tr.)

recommended by our Prophet, upon him be peace and blessings.[8] It is also expiation for sins. There is a *hadith* which says, "Receive the prayers of the ill, for their prayers are acceptable."[9]

Especially if the person who is ill is a relative, in particular parents, looking after them is an important form of worship which yields significant rewards. To please an invalid's heart and to console them is like giving alms. Fortunate is the one who pleases the easily-touched hearts of their father and mother when they are ill, and receives their prayer. Indeed, even the angels applaud saying, "How good, how blessed that is! May God reward them abundantly!" before faithful scenes of those good offspring who respond to the compassion and care of their parents—those most worthy of respect in the life of society—during their illness with perfect respect and filial kindness, showing the exaltedness of humanity.

There is great happiness and joy during an illness which arises from the kindness, pity, and compassion of those around the one who is sick; they reduce the pains of the illness to nothing. The acceptability of the prayers of the sick is of great importance. For the past thirty or forty years, I myself have prayed to be cured of the lumbago from which I suffer. However, I understood that the illness was given to me as an encouragement to prayer. Since prayer cannot be removed through prayer, that is, since prayer cannot remove itself,[10] I understood that the answer to prayers will be obtained in the Hereafter, and that illness is itself a kind of worship, for through illness one realizes one's innate impotence and seeks refuge in the Divine Court. Therefore, although I have prayed for thirty years to be healed and apparently my prayer has not been accepted, it has never occurred to me to abandon the prayer. Because illness is the occasion or reason for prayer; to be cured is not the effect of the

---

8   *al-Bukhari*, "Marda'" 4, 5; *Muslim*, "Salam" 47.

9   *Ibn Maja* "Jana'iz" 1; al-Bayhaqi, *Shu'ab al-Iman*, 6:541. (Tr.)

10   Certain illnesses encourage and are the reason for prayer. Therefore, if a prayer causes the termination of the illness, then prayer would annul the reason for it. This cannot be admitted.

prayer. If the All-Wise and Compassionate One bestows healing, He bestows it out of His pure grace.

Furthermore, if prayers are not accepted in the form we desire, it should not be said that they have not been answered. The All-Wise Creator knows better than us; He gives whatever is good for us. Sometimes in our interest He accepts our prayers for our worldly life in the name of our afterlife. In any event, a prayer that acquires sincerity due to an illness and which arises from our innate weakness, impotence, humility and need in particular, is very close to being acceptable. Illness is the means to the prayer that is sincere in this way. Both the sick who are religious and believers who look after the sick should make the most of this prayer.

The eighteenth remedy

You who are ill and have abandoned offering thanks and have now taken up complaining! Complaints arise from a right to complain. You have no rights violated, nor have you lost anything which would allow you to complain. Rather, there are numerous thanks that are obligatory for you, but you have not fulfilled them. Without performing your duties towards God Almighty, which are His rights over you, you are complaining as if you are demanding rights in a manner that is not righteous. You cannot look at others who are better off than you in health and complain. You are rather charged with looking at those who are worse than you in health, and offering thanks. If your hand is broken, look at those whose hands have been severed. If you have only one eye, look at those blind, lacking both eyes. And offer thanks to God!

Certainly, no one has the right to consider others as more advantaged than themselves in regard to bounties and to complain. And in tribulations, it is the right of all to consider those who are worse off than themselves, and thus offer thanks. This truth has been explained in a number of places in the *Risale-i Nur* with a simile, a summary of which is as follows:

A person conducts a poor wretch to the top of a minaret. At every step he gives the wretch a different gift, a different bounty. Right at the top of the minaret he gives him the largest gift. Although he deserves thanks and gratitude in return for all those various gifts, the churlish wretch forgets the gifts he has received at each step, or considers them of no importance, and without offering thanks, looks above him and begins to complain, saying: "If only this minaret had been higher, I could have climbed even further. Why isn't it as tall as that mountain over there or that other minaret?" If he begins to complain like this, what great ingratitude this is, what a great wrong!

In the same way, every human being comes into existence from nothing, and without being a rock or a tree or an animal, becomes human. Furthermore, being a Muslim is another great bounty. Most of the time, we enjoy good health and are honored with a great number of bounties. Despite all this, to complain and show impatience because we are not worthy of some bounties due to certain deficiencies pertaining to ourselves, or because we lose them through wrong choices or abuses, or because we were unable to obtain them, and thus to criticize the Divine Lordship, saying, "What have I done to cause this to happen to me?" is a spiritual sickness more disastrous than the physical one. Like fighting with a broken hand, complaint makes illness worse. The sensible person is the one who is proclaimed as,

> *Those who, when a disaster befalls them, say, "Surely we belong to God (as His creatures and servants), and surely to Him we are bound to return." (And they act accordingly)* (2: 156),

and shows patience in submission to God Almighty, so that the illness may complete its duty and depart.

The nineteenth remedy

As a term signifying God's being the Eternally Besought-of-All, while He Himself is in need of nothing, "the All-Beautiful Names" show that all the Names of the All-Gracious One of Majesty are beautiful. Among created beings, the most subtle, the most beautiful, the most comprehensive mirror that reflects God's being the Eternally Besought-of-All is life. The mirror to the beautiful is beautiful. The mirror that shows the beauties of the beautiful becomes beautiful. Just as whatever befalls the mirror through such beauty is good and beautiful, so also whatever befalls life, from the viewpoint of truth, is good, because it exhibits the beautiful imprints of the All-Beautiful Names, which are all good and beautiful.

If life passes monotonously with permanent health and appetite, it becomes a deficient mirror. Indeed, in one respect, it suggests nonexistence and nothingness, and causes weariness. It reduces the value of life, and changes the pleasure of life into distress. With the intention of passing their time quickly, out of boredom people let themselves fall into either dissipation or into distractions. They become hostile to their valuable life as if it were a prison sentence, and want to kill it, and make it pass quickly. By contrast, a life that revolves in change and action and different states makes its value felt, and enables us to recognize its importance and pleasure. Even if it is a life of troubles and misfortune, one with such a life does not want life to pass quickly. They make no complaints out of boredom; they do not utter, "Alas! The sun hasn't set yet," or, "It is still night time."

Ask a rich and idle gentleman who is living in the lap of luxury with nothing lacking, "How are you?" You will certainly hear a pathetic reply like, "Time never passes. Let's have a game of backgammon. Or let's find some other distraction to make time pass." Or else you will hear complaints arising from long-term worldly ambitions, like, "I haven't attained this; if only I had done that activity."

Then ask someone struck by disaster or a laborer or a poor man who is in hardship, "How are you?" If they are sensible, they will reply, "All thanks be to my Lord, I am well and working. If only the evening did not come so quickly, I could have finished this task! Time passes so quickly, and life goes on without stopping. Certainly, I have troubles and difficulties, but they will pass too. Everything passes quickly." In effect, such a person is saying how valuable life is and how they regret its passing. This means that they understand the pleasure and value of life which comes with hardship and labor, while ease and health make life bitter and make one desire for it to pass.

You, brother or sister Muslim, who are sick! As is explained convincingly and in detail in some other parts of the *Risale-i Nur*, know that the origin and culture of calamities and evils, and even of sins, is non-existence. As for non-existence, it is evil and darkness. It is because states like continuous ease, silence, inertia, and being sedentary are close to non-existence and nothingness that they make felt the darkness of non-existence and cause distress. As for action and change, they are existence and make existence felt. And existence is pure good, and it is light.

Since this is a reality, your illness has been sent to your body as a guest so that it will carry out many duties like purifying your valuable life, and strengthening and developing it, as well as making other members and faculties of your body turn in assistance towards the part of you that is unwell, and displaying the imprints of various Names of the All-Wise Maker. God willing, the illness will carry out its duties quickly and depart. And it will say to good health, "Now you come, and stay permanently in my place, and carry out your duties. This house is yours. Remain here in a good condition."

The twentieth remedy

You who are sick and seeking a remedy for your ills! Illness is of two kinds. One kind is real; the other is imaginary. As for the real kind, the All-Wise Healer of Majesty has stored up in His mighty pharmacy of the earth a remedy for every illness. Without illness, how can those remedies be known and enjoyed? The Religion requires that medicines should be used in treatment, but we should know that their effect and the cure are from God Almighty. It is He Who gives the cure, and it is He Who provides the medicine.

Following the recommendations of skilful, God-conscious doctors is an important form of treatment. For most illnesses arise from abuses, a lack of abstinence, extravagance, vice, dissipation, and indifference and a lack of care. A God-conscious doctor will certainly give advice and orders that are not contrary to Islamic precepts. They will forbid abuses and extravagance, and give consolation. The sick person has confidence in their recommendations and consolation, and the illness wanes, giving a feeling of relief in place of distress.

But when it comes to illnesses that are imaginary, the most effective medicine of all is to give it no importance. The more importance is given to it, the more it grows and swells. If no importance is given, the illness lessens and fades away. The more bees are disturbed, the more they swarm around a person's head, while if they are paid no attention, they disperse. Also, the more attention one pays to a piece of string waving in front of one's eyes in the darkness, the more it disturbs one and causes one to flee from it like a madman. While if you pay it no attention, you can see that it is an ordinary bit of string and not a snake, and you will laugh at your fear and anxiety.

If the groundless worry about one's health continues for a long time, it is transformed into reality. It is an evil ailment for the nervous and those given to groundless fears and worries; such people make a mountain out of a molehill and their morale is destroyed. In particular, if they encounter unkind and unfair "half" doctors, their worries are provoked and increase. If they are rich, they lose their wealth, or else they lose their wits, or their health.

The twenty-first remedy

You, brother or sister in faith, who are sick! You are suffering physical pain because of your illness, but a significant spiritual pleasure which will remove the effect of your physical pain surrounds you. For if you have a father, mother, or relatives, their most pleasurable compassion towards you, which you have long forgotten, will be awakened and you will see again their kind looks which you received in childhood. In addition, the friends around you who have remained veiled and hidden will look again towards you with love through the attraction of illness. In the face of these, your physical pain is infinitesimal. Also, those whom you serve proudly and from whom you try to receive appreciation now serve you kindly due to your illness, and thus you have become a master of your masters. Furthermore, since you have attracted towards yourself the fellow feeling and human tenderness of people, you have found many helpful friends and kind companions who expect nothing in return. Again, you have received from your illness the order to rest from many exhausting duties, and you are taking a rest. Certainly, in the face of these spiritual pleasures, your minor pain should lead you to thanks, not to complaint.

The twenty-second remedy

You, brother or sister in faith, who suffer a severe illness such as paralysis! Firstly, I give you the good news that for believers paralysis is regarded as blessed. I have long heard this from saintly people, but I did not know the reason. Now, one reason occurs to me as follows:

In order to obtain the approval and good pleasure of God Almighty, and to be saved from the great dangers that this world poses to the spiritual life, and to attain eternal happiness, the people of God have chosen to follow two principles:

The first is contemplation of death. Thinking of the world as transitory and realizing that they too are transient guests in the world who have many duties, they work for the eternal life in this way.

The second: In order to be saved from the dangers of the carnal, evil-commanding soul and blind passions, they have tried to kill the evil-commanding soul through austerity, religious exercises, and asceticism.

And you, my brother or sister, who have lost the health of half your body! Without choosing to do so, you have been given these two principles, which are the cause of happiness, so that your body continually warns you against the fleeting nature of the world and reminds you that humans are mortal. The world cannot drown you anymore, nor can heedlessness close your eyes. And certainly, the carnal, evil-commanding soul cannot deceive someone in the state of half a person by vile lusts and animal appetites; that person is quickly saved from the trials of the evil-commanding soul.

Thus, through belief in and submission to God and reliance on Him, a believer can benefit in a short time from a severe illness like paralysis, rather than undergoing the severe trials of the saints. Thus an illness that is so severe becomes an exceedingly modest exchange for these gains.

The twenty-third remedy

You who are ill and unhappy, alone and a stranger! While your isolation and exile together with your illness arouse sympathy in the hardest hearts and attract kindness and compassion to you, certainly they will also attract the All-Compassionate Creator's compassion towards you, which is certain to be a substitute for the sympathy and compassion of everything else. It is He Who presents Himself to us at the start of all but one of the *suras* of the Qur'an with the Attributes of "All-Merciful and All-Compassionate." Through one gleam of His Compassion, He causes all mothers to nurture their young with wonderful tenderness, and through one manifestation of His Mercy every spring, He fills the face of the earth with bounties. Also, with all its wonders, Paradise, which is the abode of eternal happiness, constitutes a single manifestation of His Mercy. Thus, your relation to Him through belief, your recognition of Him and entreating Him through the voice of helplessness that is found in your illness, and your loneliness in exile will surely attract His mercy towards you.

Since He exists and He looks to you, everything exists for you. Those who are truly alone and in exile are those who have no relation to Him through belief and submission, or who attach no importance to that relation.

The twenty-fourth remedy

You who tend innocent, sick children or the elderly who are like innocent children! Before you is an important commodity for the Hereafter. Carry out these tasks with zeal and endeavor! In the illnesses of innocent children there are many instances of wisdom pertaining to their worldly life. For instance, their illnesses are like exercises and drills for their delicate bodies, and the inoculations and training of the Lord, so that they may be able to withstand the tumults and upheavals of the world in the future. As is accepted by verifying scholars, like expiations for sins in adults, the illnesses of innocent children are also inoculations which will serve their spiritual life, their spiritual purification and development in the future or in the Hereafter. In addition, the merits ensuing from such illnesses are recorded in the notebook of the good deeds of the parents, and particularly of the mother who, out of compassion, prefers the health of her child to her own.

As for looking after the elderly, it is accurately reported from our Prophet, upon him be peace and blessings, and has been established by many historical events, that in addition to bringing mighty rewards, receiving the prayers of the elderly, and especially that of parents, and making their hearts happy and serving them faithfully is the means to happiness both in this world and in the Hereafter.[11] And there are many experiences that establish that a child who perfectly obeys his elderly parents will receive the same treatment from his or her children, and that a child who wounds his or her parents will not only be punished in the Hereafter, but will also be subject to many disasters in this world. Not only looking after relatives who are elderly or innocent children, but also serving willingly any believing sick person, especially if that one is in need of us—since there is true brotherhood coming from belief—is a requirement of being a Muslim.

The twenty-fifth remedy

You, brother and sister Muslims, who are ill! If you desire a most beneficial, truly pleasurable, and sacred medicine, which is the cure for every illness, develop your belief! That is, through repentance and seeking God's forgiveness for your sins, and the five daily Prayers, and

---

[11]   *al-Bukhari*, "Adab" 1–6,; *Muslim*, "Birr" 1–6, 9, 10; *at-Tirmidhi*, "Da'awat" 110.

other duties of worship, apply to your illnesses belief—that sacred cure—and the medicine it provides.

Indeed, due to the love of this world and attachment to it, it is as if the worldly people have a sick worldly existence as big as the world. We have convincingly explained in many parts of the *Risale-i Nur* that belief immediately heals that sick existence, which, like the world itself, is subject to the blows of death and separation and "riddled" with wounds and bruises. I cut short the discussion here not to weary you.

As for the medicine of belief, it shows its effect when you carry out your religious obligations as far as is possible. Heedlessness, dissipation, carnal desires, and religiously forbidden amusements prevent the effectiveness of that remedy. Since illness removes heedlessness, reduces the appetites, and prevents one from partaking in religiously unlawful pleasures, take advantage of it. Apply the sacred medicines and lights of true belief through repentance, seeking God's forgiveness, and prayers, and supplications.

May Almighty God restore you to health and make your illnesses expiation for your sins. Amen. Amen. Amen.

> They say: *"All praise and gratitude are for God, Who has guided us to this. If God had not guided us, we would certainly not have found the right way. The Messengers of our Lord did indeed come with the truth."* (7: 43)

> All-Glorified are You. We have no knowledge save what You have taught us. Surely You are the All-Knowing, the All-Wise.

> O God! Bestow blessings on our master Muhammad, the medicine for hearts and their cure, the good health of bodies and their healing, the light of eyes and their light, and on his Family and Companions, and bestow on them peace.

DEFINITION OF ISLAMIC TERMS

The following Islamic terms are important for understanding the present study:

Al-Fatiha: The Opening (the first chapter of the Qur'an)

As-Shafi: The Healer. It is one of the 99 Divine Names in the Qur'an.

Ayat: Verse of Qur'an.

Dhikr: Literally means «remembrance» or «invocation». It is remembering God with certain invocations by tongue or by heart. It includes the repetition of Divine Names. Activities that maintain awareness of God in a Muslim is are considered *dhikr*.

Du'a: Verbal formal and informal supplication. An extensive explanation is provided later on in this section.

Fard: Literally means obligatory. It is performing the practices that were obliged onto Muslims by God in both the Qur'an and hadith.

Hadith: Sayings of the Prophet Muhammad, peace be upon him. It is a branch of *sunnah*. The hadith has been memorized or written, collected, and compiled by the Prophet's companions, family members, and scholars. When *hadith* are recorded, the chain of narrators (*isnad*), pious people who have memorized or written the *hadiths*, is also recorded for credibility purposes. The authenticity of a *hadith* is given strict consideration. There are six *hadith* compilations that are generally accepted by Sunni scholars as authentic. The first complete compilation was done by Muhammed ibn-Ismail Al-Bukahri (810-870). The other five were by Imam Muslim (d.875), Ibn Maja (d.886), Abu Daud (d.888), At-Tirmidhi (d.892), and An-Nasai (d.915). Shiites accept the hadith collection books of Mohammad Yaqub

Al-Kulayni (d.950), Shaikh Saduq (d.1013), Abu Jafar al-Tusi (d.1274).

Masjid: Arabic word for mosque. It is the building where Muslims gather for congregational prayers.

Peace be upon him: It is a tradition in Islam to mention this after the name of any prophet. It is a sign of respect to say this phrase after Prophet Muhammad's name is mentioned.

Qu'ran: Literally means "recitation". It is the holy book of Muslims. Muslims consider this book to be a revelation from God. It is written and recited in the Arabic language, although translations have been made to many languages. The original Arabic text has been recorded and memorized by millions of Muslims. Most Muslims know at least a few chapters of the Qur'an. Practicing Muslims read or recite some chapters daily.

Sadaqa: Arabic word for charity.

Salat: The five daily obligatory prayers. An extensive explanation is provided later on in this section.

Sharia: the body of Islamic law. The term means "way" or "path"; it is the legal framework within which the public and some private aspects of life are regulated for those living in a legal system based on Islamic principles of jurisprudence. *Sharia* deals with every aspect of daily life, including politics, economics, banking, business law, contract law, sexuality, and social issues.

Shifa: Arabic word for healing or cure.

Surah: Chapter of the Qur'an.

Sunnah: Literally means "the way", therefore meaning the way of the Prophet, i.e., the actions and sayings (*hadiths*) of Prophet Muhammad, peace be upon him, and the actions of others approved by the Prophet. In Islamic jurisprudence, the *sunnah* is the second source of religion. Just like the hadith, the *sunnah* of Prophet Muhammad, peace be upon him, has been recorded, memorized, and transmitted from generation to generation with a chain of reliable narrators.

Tibb Nabawi: The medicine of Prophet Muhammad, peace be upon
   him. It includes how the Prophet treated patients, the objects
   he used, and his recommendations for treating patients.

Wudu (ablution): this is the physical preparation for the five daily ritual prayers. It begins with washing the hands, mouth, nose,
   face, and arms, followed by wiping the hair with a wet hand,
   cleaning the ears, rubbing the neck with a wet hand, and ends
   with washing the feet. This must be performed before the *salat*,
   Qur'anic reading, and other religious activities.

Zakat: Arabic word for alms, one of the five obligations of every finan-
   cially able Muslim.

Appendixes

APPENDIXES

APPENDIX B: DEMOGRAPHICS SURVEY

1. Gender
   a) male
   b) female

2. Age _____

3. Marital status:
   a) single
   b) married
   c) divorced
   d) widow
   e) other

4. Level of education
   a) Primary school
   b) High school
   c) College graduate
   d) Master degree or above
   e) Illiterate

5. Occupation _____

6. Nationality _____

APPENDIX C: PREMINILARY SURVEY

Patient No._____   Trial no._____

Date_____

1. Depressed (0 is not depressed and 10 is most depressed)

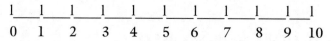

2. Anxious (0 is not anxious and 10 is most anxious)

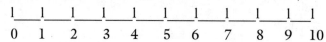

3. Angry with God (0 is not angry at all and 10 is very angry)

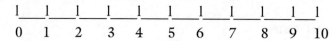

4. Lonely (0 is not lonely at all and 10 is extremely lonely)

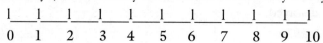

5. Submissive to the Will of God
   a) yes
   b) no

6. Hopeful (0 is not hopeful at all and 10 is extremely hopeful)

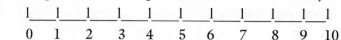

7. Despair (0 is not despairing at all and 10 is extreme despair)

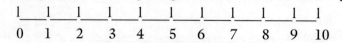

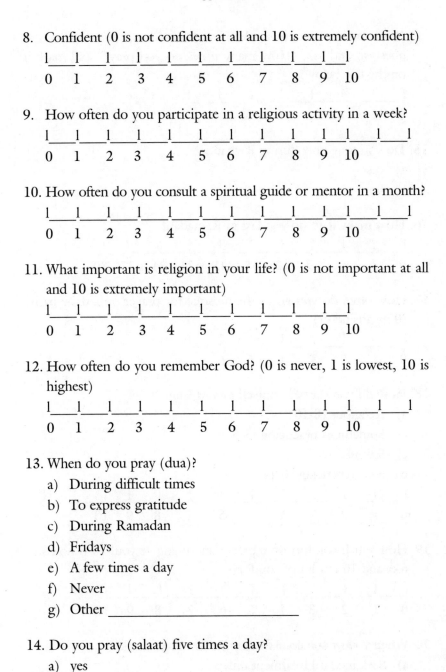

8. Confident (0 is not confident at all and 10 is extremely confident)

   |___|___|___|___|___|___|___|___|___|___|
   0   1   2   3   4   5   6   7   8   9   10

9. How often do you participate in a religious activity in a week?

   |___|___|___|___|___|___|___|___|___|___|___|
   0   1   2   3   4   5   6   7   8   9   10

10. How often do you consult a spiritual guide or mentor in a month?

    |___|___|___|___|___|___|___|___|___|___|___|
    0   1   2   3   4   5   6   7   8   9   10

11. What important is religion in your life? (0 is not important at all and 10 is extremely important)

    |___|___|___|___|___|___|___|___|___|
    0   1   2   3   4   5   6   7   8   9   10

12. How often do you remember God? (0 is never, 1 is lowest, 10 is highest)

    |___|___|___|___|___|___|___|___|___|___|___|
    0   1   2   3   4   5   6   7   8   9   10

13. When do you pray (dua)?
    a) During difficult times
    b) To express gratitude
    c) During Ramadan
    d) Fridays
    e) A few times a day
    f) Never
    g) Other _____

14. Do you pray (salaat) five times a day?
    a) yes
    b) no

(If the answer is no, then ask the next question. If yes, skip the next question and ask, "How many times do you pray?" and mark it on the line below.)

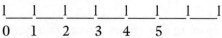

0 1 2 3 4 5

15. Do you pray only during Ramadan?
    a) yes
    b) no

16. How many days do you fast in Ramadan?

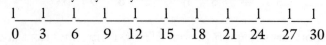

0 3 6 9 12 15 18 21 24 27 30

17. How often do you go to the mosque for prayer on a daily basis? (0 means never)

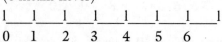

0 1 2 3 4 5 6

18. How do you classify yourself as a Muslim?
    a) Religious (8-10)
    b) Sometimes practicing (3-5)
    c) Spiritual (6-7)
    d) Non practicing (0-1)

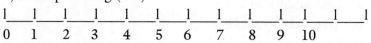

0 1 2 3 4 5 6 7 8 9 10

19. How much comfort does prayer and dua give you? (0 is no comfort and 10 is a lot of comfort)

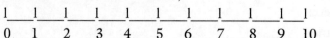

0 1 2 3 4 5 6 7 8 9 10

20. When you or someone from your family gets sick:
    a) Seek medical treatment only
    b) Seek medical treatment and pray

c) Pray only
d) Never
e) Other _____

21. Do you give Zakat?
    a) yes
    b) no

22. Do you give sadaqa?
    a) yes
    b) no

23. How often do you give sadaqa?
    a) once a week
    b) once a month
    c) quarterly
    d) other _____

24. How often do you read the Qur'an or religious books?
    a) Daily (8-10)
    b) few times a week (5-7)
    c) weekly (2-4)
    d) monthly (1)
    e) never (0)
    f) other_____

|___|___|___|___|___|___|___|___|___|___|
0   1   2   3   4   5   6   7   8   9 10

25. How often to you contemplate?

|___|___|___|___|___|___|___|___|___|___|
0   1   2   3   4   5   6   7   8   9 10

APPENDIX D: RELIGIOUS TEXT

Chapter 1: *Al-Fatiha* (The Opening)

بِسْمِ اللهِ الرَّحْمَنِ الرَّحِيمِ

الْحَمْدُ للهِ رَبِّ الْعَالَمِينَ الرَّحْمَنِ الرَّحِيمِ مَالِكِ يَوْمِ الدِّينَ

إِيَّاكَ نَعْبُدُ وَإِيَّاكَ نَسْتَعِينُ اهْدِنَا الصِّرَاطَ الْمُسْتَقِيمَ صِرَاطَ

الَّذِينَ أَنْعَمْتَ عَلَيْهِمْ غَيْرِ الْمَغْضُوبِ عَلَيْهِمْ وَلاَ الضَّالِّينَ

Chapter 2:256: *Ayatul Kursi* (Verse of the Throne)

اللهُ لاَ إِلَهَ إِلاَّ هُوَ الْحَيُّ الْقَيُّومُ لاَ تَأْخُذُهُ سِنَةٌ وَلاَ نَوْمٌ لَّهُ مَا

فِي السَّمَاوَاتِ وَمَا فِي الأَرْضِ مَن ذَا الَّذِي يَشْفَعُ عِنْدَهُ إِلاَّ

بِإِذْنِهِ يَعْلَمُ مَا بَيْنَ أَيْدِيهِمْ وَمَا خَلْفَهُمْ وَلاَ يُحِيطُونَ بِشَيْءٍ مِّنْ

عِلْمِهِ إِلاَّ بِمَا شَاءَ وَسِعَ كُرْسِيُّهُ السَّمَاوَاتِ وَالأَرْضَ وَلاَ

يَؤُودُهُ حِفْظُهُمَا وَهُوَ الْعَلِيُّ الْعَظِيمُ

Chapter 113: *Al-Falaq* (The Daybreak)

قُلْ أَعُوذُ بِرَبِّ الْفَلَقِ مِن شَرِّ مَا خَلَقَ وَمِن شَرِّ غَاسِقٍ إِذَا

وَقَبَ وَمِن شَرِّ غَاسِقٍ إِذَا وَقَبَ وَمِن شَرِّ النَّفَّاثَاتِ فِي الْعُقَدِ

وَمِن شَرِّ حَاسِدٍ إِذَا حَسَدَ

Chapter 114: An-Naas (Humankind)

قُلْ أَعُوذُ بِرَبِّ النَّاسِ مَلِكِ النَّاسِ إِلَهِ النَّاسِ مِن شَرِّ

الْوَسْوَاسِ الْخَنَّاسِ الَّذِي يُوَسْوِسُ فِي صُدُورِ النَّاسِ

Appendix E: Non-Religious Text

السياسة على لسان الحيوان

''كليلة ودمنة'' التي كتبها الحكيم الهندي ونقلها للعربية ابن المقفع منذ قرون طويلة تم إعدادها الآن كمسلسل كرتون للأطفال يحمل اسم ''دنيا الغابة''، يتم عرضه في رمضان الحالي على عدة قنوات فضائية.

المسلسل يقع في ٣٠ حلقة مدة كل حلقة ٦ دقائق ، ويُذاع في دول الخليج العربي الست، وهو من إخراج الدكتورة تماضر محمد نجيب: الأستاذة بمعهد السينما بأكاديمية الفنون المصرية ، والتي شاركت أيضاً في إعداد السيناريو مع السينارست أحمد علام، وقد أخرجت قبل ذلك ١٢٠ فقرة حية من برنامج ‹‹افتح يا سمسم›› الذي أنتجته مؤسسة الإنتاج البرامجي المشترك لدول الخليج العربي.

ونسأل د. تماضر: لماذا وقع الاختيار على هذه القصص التراثية لتنفذ فى شكل مسلسل كرتونى للأطفال؟

تقول الدكتورة تماضر: قصص ‹‹كليلة ودمنة›› هي عبارة عن مواعظ ونصائح أخلاقية وسياسية وثقافية ودينية، تصلح لكل زمان ومكان، والأطفال لا يحبون النصائح المباشرة؛ ولهذا اخترنا أن تكون على لسان الحيوان تماماً كما هي القصة الأصلية؛ حيث كان الحكيم دايدبا (الهندي) يحكي للحاكم الظالم القصص على لسان الحيوانات؛ حتى يوصل إليه المعنى الذي يريد إيصاله له بشكل غير مباشر، وينتقل إلى عالم الحيوان من خلال الشخصيات الرئيسية في الغابة، وهي (كليلة) وهو ثعلب طيب القلب و (دمنة) وهو ثعلب أيضاً لئيم يدبر المؤمرات لبقية الحيوانات ويسعى دائماً للسلطة والسيطرة، وهناك أيضاً (الأسد) وهو ملك الغابة، والقرد (ميمون) طيب القلب، والفيل، والنمر والهدهد، والجمل والثور، وقد تحكي كل حلقة قصة كاملة أو قد تحتاج القصة الطويلة لأكثر من حلقة.

هل يمكن أن نعود في عصر الفضائيات إلى القصص التراثية؟

- الخير والشر موجود منذ بدء الخليقة وحتى الآن، لكن لا يمكن أن ننقل الواقع كما هو للأطفال، ولا حتى للكبار، بل من خلال شخصيات محببة إلى قلب الطفل كالحيوانات، وأطفالنا أذكياء جداً، ونحن الذين نتصور أنهم أغبياء وتظهر في برامج الكرتون الأجنبي عندما نترجم هذه المشاهد التي يراها الطفل ونحكيها له، في حين أن الأطفال الآن لديهم ثقافة مرئية أو ما يسمى بثقافة الصورة، ويدرك الطفل لماذا يقفز هذا الشخص ويجري الآخر ويبكي الثالث دون أن يكون الفيلم الكرتوني بلغته الأصلية، فبإمكانه اكتشاف الأحداث وربطها ببعضها بأفضل مما نتصور، ثم لماذا لا يثور التساؤل مع مسلسلات ديزني الكرتونية عن الغابة وحيواناتها ويثور حين نصوغ نحن قصص الحيوان بما يتفق مع قيمنا لتصبح الغابة رمزا بدلاً من أفلام أمريكا التي تحمل قيم صراعية سافرة تجعل الدنيا غابة حقيقية؟!

APPENDIX F: POST-SURVEY SURVEY

Patient No._____   Trial no._____

Date_____

1. Do you feel more comfort than before you prayed?
    a) yes
    b) no

2. How comfortable do you feel? (0 is for not comfortable and 10 is for extremely comfortable)

0	1	2	3	4	5	6	7	8	9	10

3. Do you feel stronger spiritually?
    a) yes
    b) no

4. How stronger do you feel spiritually? (0 is not stronger at all and 10 is very strong)

0	1	2	3	4	5	6	7	8	9	10

5. What is the state of your mind? (0 is very clear and 10 is not clear at all)

0	1	2	3	4	5	6	7	8	9	10

6. How often would you like an imam to come and pray for you on a weekly basis? (0 is never. 1 is once a week and 10 is ten times a week)

0	1	2	3	4	5	6	7	8	9	10

7. Would you like family and friends to pray for you?
   a) yes
   b) no

8. How often would you like your family and friends to pray for you?
   (0 is never. 1 is once a week and 10 is ten times a week)

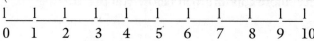

   | 0 | 1 | 2 | 3 | 4 | 5 | 6 | 7 | 8 | 9 | 10 |

9. Do you feel closer to God?
   a) yes
   b) no

10. Would you pray for people who you know are ill?
    a) yes
    b) no

11. Do you feel God's presence?
    a) yes
    b) no

12. Does prayer affect your physical condition?
    a) yes
    b) no

13. Do you believe that prayer affects you positively?
    a) yes
    b) no

14. Has praying increased your reliance upon God?
    a) yes
    b) no

15. Would you recommend prayer to another patient?
    a) yes
    b) no

16. If the imam does not come, will you pray or read Qur'an by yourself?
a) yes
b) no

17. How often will you pray daily? (0 is never and 10 is ten times a day)

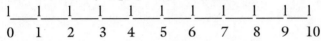

0 1 2 3 4 5 6 7 8 9 10

18. How many pages of Qur'an will you read or recite in a day? (0 is
never and 10 is ten pages a day)

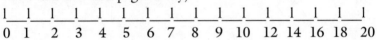

0 1 2 3 4 5 6 7 8 9 10 12 14 16 18 20

19. Will you continue to pray and recite Qur'an after you are discharged?
a) yes
b) no

SOURCES

Adib, Salim M. "From the Biomedical Model to the Islamic Alternative: A Brief Overview of Medical Practices in the Contemporary Arab World." *Social Science & Medicine* 58, no.4 (2004): 697-702.

Al- Dhahabi, Shams Ul-Din. *Al-Tibb An-Nawawi* (Medicine of the Prophet). Riyadh: Maktabat Nizar Mustafa al-Baz, 1996.

Al-Ghazali, Abu-Hamid. *Ihyay-I Ulumudden* (The Revival of Religious Science). Translated by Mehmet Emre. Istanbul: Bedir Publications, 1976.

Al-Ghazali, Abu Hamid. *Worship in Islam*. Translated by E. E. Calverley. New Jersey: Gorgias Press, 2004.

Al-Habib, T. *Al-'Ilajun Nafs Wa Al-'Ilajul Bil* Qur'an (The Medicine of the Soul and The Medicine with the Qur'an). Riyadh: Jarees Publishing, 1995.

Al-Jawziyyah, Ibn Al-Qayyim. *Healing with the Medicine of the Prophet*. Translated by Jalal Abu Al-rab, ed. Abdul R. Abdullah. Riyadh: Darussalam Publications, 1999.

Al-Kandari, Yagoub Yousif. "Religosity and Its Relation to Blood Pressure among Selected Kuwaitis." *Journal of Biosocial Science* 35, no.3 (2003): 463-472.

Al-Qushayri, Abd Al-Karim. *Principles of Sufism*. Translated by B.R. Von Schlegell. New York: Mizan Press, 1990.

Al-Razi, Abu Bakr Z. *The Spiritual Physick of Rhazes*. Translated by Arthur J. Arberry. New York: Paragon Book Gallery, Ltd: 1950.

Al-Suyuti, Jalal Ad-Din. *Tibb-ul Nabbi* (Medicine of the Prophet). Translated by Cyril Elgood. London: Ta-Ha Publishers, 1962.

Al-Tabari, Abu Ja`far M. *Jami`al Bayan `An Ta'wil Al-Qur'an*. Beirut: Dar ul-Fikr Publications, 1995.

Al-Tharshi, Adnan. *As-Salaat war-Riyadhiyya wal-*Badan (Prayer, Exercise, and the Body). Beirut: Maktabatul Islami, 1992.

Arasteh, Abdol R. and Anees A. Sheikh. "Sufism: The Way to Universal Self." In *Eastern and Western Approaches to Healing: Ancient Wisdom and Modern Knowledge*, ed. Anees A. Sheikh and Katharina S. Sheikh. New York: John Wiley & Sons, 1989.

Athar, Shahid, ed. Islamic Perspectives in Medicine: *Achievements and Contemporary Issues*. New York: Kazi Publications, 1996.

Balaskas, Janet. *New Life: The Book of Exercise for Child Birth*. London: Sidwick and Jackson, 1979.

Benson, H., other authors. (2006). Study of the Therapeutic Effects of Intercessory Prayer (STEP) in cardiac bypass patients: A multi-center randomized trial of uncertainty and certainty of receiving intercessory prayer. *American Heart Journal, 151*, 934-42.

Benson, Herbert. *Timeless Healing: The Power and Biology of Belief*. New York: Scribner Press, 1996.

Bussing, Amdt, Thomas Ostermann, and Peter F. Matthiessen. "Roles of Religion and Spirituality in Medical Patients: Confirmatory Results with the SpREUK Questionnaire." *Health and Quality of Life Outcomes* 3, no.10 (2005): 1-10.

Cloninger, C. Robert. "Fostering Spirituality and Well-Being in Clinical Practice." *Psychiatric Annals* 36, no.3 (2006): 1-6.

Cotton, Slan P., Ellen G. Levine, Cory M. Fitzpatrick, Kristin H. Dold, Elisabeth Targ. "Exploring the Relationships among Spiritual Well-Being, Quality of Life, and Psychological Adjustment in Women with Breast Cancer." *Psycho-Oncology* 8, no.5 (1999): 429-438.

Dafni, Amots. "On the Typology of the Worship Status of Sacred Trees with a Special Reference to the Middle East." *Jounal of Ethnobiology and Ethnomedicine* 2, no.26 (2006): 1-14

Daujat, Jean. *Prayer*. Translated by Martin Murphy. New York: Hawthorn Books, 1964.

Delong, William R. "Scientific and Pastoral Perspectives on Intercessory Prayer". *Journal of Health Care Chaplaincy* 7, no.1/2 (1998): 63-71.

Dogan, Mebrure. "Duanin Psikolojik ve Psikoterapik Etkileri (The Effects of Prayer on Psychology and Psychotherapy)." Ph.D diss., Cumhuriyet University, Turkey, 1997.

Dols, Michael W. *Medieval Islamic Medicine*. Berkley, CA: University of California Press, 1985.

Dossey, Larry. "Prayer, Medicine and Science: The New Dialogue." In *Scientific and Pastoral Perspectives on Intercessory Prayer: An Exchange between Larry Dossey, M.D. and Health Care Chaplains*, ed. Larry Vandecreek, 661-671. New York: The Haworth Press Inc, 1998.

Cilaci, Osman, ed. *Islam Ansiklopedisi* (Encyclopedia of Islam) vol. 9.1964.

Deylemi, E. F. "Dua." In *Hadis Ansiklopedesi* (Hadith Encyclopedia) vol 5, ed. Ibrahim Canan. Istanbul: Akcag Publishing, 1993.

Ferraro, Kenneth F. & Cynthia M. Albrecht-Jensen. "Does Religion Influence Adult Health?" *Journal for the Scientific Study of Religion* 30, no.2 (Jun 1991): 193-202.

Gülen, M. Fethullah. *Questions and Answers about Faith*. Translated by Ali Ünal. New Jersey: Fountain Publications, 1993.

Helm, Hughes M, Judith C. Hays, Elizabeth P. Flint, Harold G. Koenig, and Dan G. Blazer. "Does Private Religious Activity Prolong Survival? A Six-Year Follow-up Study of 3,851 Older Adults." *The Journal of Gerontology Series A: Biological Sciences and Medical Sciences* 55, no.7 (2000): 400-405.

Hermansen, Marcia. "Dimensions of Islamic Religious Healing." In *Religion and Healing in America*, ed. Linda L. Barnes & Susan S. Sered, 407-422. New York: Oxford University Press, 2005.

Hodge, David .R. "A Template for Spiritual Assessment: A Review of the JCAHO Requirements and Guidelines for Implementation." *Social Work* 51, no.4 (2006), 317-326.

Hummer, Robert. A., Richard G Rogers, Charles B Nam, and Christophet G Ellison. "Religious Involvement and U.S. Adult Mortality." *Demography* 36, no.2 (1999): 273-285.

Ibn Kathir, Ismail. *Tafsir Ibn Kathir* (Qur'ani Commentary of Ibn Kathir). Beirut: Darul Qalam.

Ismail, Hanif, John Wright, Penny Rhodes, and Neil Small. "Religious Beliefs About Causes and Treatment of Epilepsy." *British Journal of General Practice* 55, no.510 (Jan 2005): 26-31.

James, William. *The Varieties of Religious Experience.* New York: New York University Books, 1963.

Joint Commission on Accreditation of Health Organizations (JCAHO). *Comprehensive Acrreditation Manual for Hospitals (CAMH): The Official Handbook.* Oakbrook Terrace, 1999.

Jonas, Wayne B and Cindy C. Crawford. "Science and Spiritual Healing: A Critical Review of Spiritual Healing, 'Energy' Medicine, and Intentionality." *Alternative Therapies in Health and Medicine* 9, no.2 (Mar 2003): 56-61.

Kark, J D., G Shemi, Y Friedlander, O Martin, O Manor and S H. Blondheim. "Does Religious Observance Promote Health? Mortality in Secular vs Religious Kibbutzim in Israel." American Journal of Public Health 86, no.3 (1996): 341-346.

Kayiklik, Hasan. H. *"Kuran'ın Işığinda Inanan Insanın Duasına Psikolojik Yaklaşımlar* (Psychological Approaches of a Believer's Du'a in the Light of the Qur'an)". Ph.D. diss., Çukurova University, Turkey, 1994.

Kizmaz, Mustafa. "Dinin Hastalar Uzerindeki Etkisi (The Effects of Religion on Patients)." Şanliurfa, Turkey: Harran University, 1998.

Koenig, HG, Linda K. George, Judith C. Hayes, David B. Larson, H J. Cohen, and Dan G. Blazer. "Attendance at Religious Services, Interleukin-6, and Other Biological Parameters of Immune Function in Older Adults." *International Journal of Psychiatry in Medicine* 27, no.3 (1997): 233-250.

Koenig, Harold G., Linda K. George, HJ Cohen, Judith C. Hays, David B. Larson, and Dan G. Blazer. "The Relationship between Religious Activities and Cigarette Smoking in Older Adults." *Journals of Gerontology Series, A: Biological Sciences and Medical Sciences* 53, no.6 (1998): 426-434.

Koenig, HG, Linda K. George, Judith C. Hayes, David B. Larson, H J. Cohen, and Dan G. Blazer. "The Relationship between Religious

Activities and Blood Pressure in Older Adults." *International Journal of Psychiatry Medicine* 28, no. 2 (1998): 189-213.

Levin, Jeff S, Vanderpool, Harold Y. *Religious Factors in Physical Health and the Prevention of Illness*. Prevention in Human Services 9, no.2 (1991): 41-64.

Levin, Jeff. God, Faith, and Health: Exploring the Spirituality-Healing Connection. New York: John Wiley & Sons Inc, 2001.

Mueller, Paul S, David J. Plevak, ad Teresa A. Rummans. "Religious Involvement, Spirituality, and Medicine: Implications for Clinical Practice." *Mayo Clinic Proceedings* 76, no.12 (2001):1225-1235.

Nasr, Seyyed H. *Sufi Essays*, 2nd Ed. Albany: State University of New York Press, 1991.

Nawawi, Abu Zakariyyah. *Riyadus Saliheen* (Gardens of Righteousness). Translated by Mehmet Emre. Istanbul: Bedir Publications, 1978.

Nursi, Said. *The Letters*. Translated by Sukran Vahide. Istanbul: Sozler Publishing, 1994.

Nursi, Said. *The Words*. Translated by Huseyin Akarsu. New Jersey: Light Publications, 2005.

O'Connor, Patrick G., Nicholas P.Pronk, Agnes Tan, and Robin R. Whitebird. "Characteristics of Adults Who Use Prayer as an Alternative Therapy." *American Journal of Health Promotion* 19, no.5 (2005):369-375.

Puchalski, Christina M. "The Role of Spirituality in Health Care." *BUMC Proceedings* 14, no.4 (2001): 352-357.

Qutb, Sayyid. *Fi Zilal Al-Qur'an* (In the Shade of the Qur'an). Cairo: Dar Us-Sharuuq Publications, 1976.

Rahman, Fazlur. *Health and Medicine in the Islamic Tradition*. New York: The Crossroad Publishing Company, 1987.

Razali, Salleh M., Kassim Aminah, and Umeed A. Khan. "Religious-Cultural Psychotherapy in the Management of Anxiety Patients." *Transcultural Psychiatry* 39, no.1 (2002): 130-136.

Reza, Mohammed F., Yuji Urakami, and Yukio Mano. "Evaluation of a New Physical Exercise Taken from *Salat* (Prayer) As A Short-Duration and Frequent Physical Activity in the Rehabilitation of

Geriatric and Disabled Patients." *Annals of Saudi Medicine* 22, no.3-4 (2002): 177-180.

Rasanayagam, J. (2006). Healing with spirits and the formation of Muslim selfhood in post-Soviet Uzbekistan. *Journal of the Royal Anthropological Institute, 12,* 377-493.

Ruland, Vernon. *Sacred Lies and Silences: A Psychology of Religious Disguise.* Collegeville, MN: The Liturgical Press, 1994.

Sayin, Esma. "Namazin Karakter Gelisimi Uzerine Etkisi (The Effects of Prayer on Character Development)." Masters thesis. unpublished Master thesis. Bursa, Turkey: Uludağ University, 2003.

Schimell, Annemarie. "Some Aspects of Mystical Prayer in Islam". *Die Welt des Islams New Ser* 2, no.2 (1952): 112-125.

Sengers, Gerda. *Women and Demons: Cult Healing in Islamic Egypt.* Boston: Brill, 2003.

Seriati, Ali. *Dua.* Translated by Kerim Guney. Birlesik Yayincilik: Istanbul, 1993.

Soysaldi, H. Mehmet. *Kur'an-ı Kerime Göre Dua.* Istanbul: Yeni Ufuklar Neşriyat, İstanbul, 1996.

Stavros, George S. "An Empirical Study of the Impact of Contemplative Prayer on Psychological, Relational and Spiritual Wellbeing." Ph.D. diss,. Denver University, 1997.

Steffen, Patrick R, James A. Blumenthal, Alan L. Hinderliter, and Andrew Sherwood. "Religious Coping, Ethnicity, and Ambulatory Blood Pressure." *Psychosomatic Medicine* 63, no.4 (2001): 523-530.

Ünal, Ali. *The Qur'an: An Annotated Interpretation in Modern English.* NJ: Tughra Books, 2006.

Wood, Christopher. Mood Change and Perceptions of Vitality: a Comparison of the Effects of Relaxation, Visualization, and Yoga. *Journal of the Royal Society of Medicine* 86, no.5 (1993) 254-258.

Yazır, Elmalılı H. *Hak Dini Kur'an Dili* (The True Religion, The Language of the Qur'an). Ph.D. diss,. Çukurova University, Turkey, 1960.

Yousif, Ahmad F. "Islamic Medicine and Health Care: Historical and Contemporary Views." *The Park Ridge Center Bulletin* 25 (Feb 2002): 5-6.

Zuhayli, Vehbe. Islam Fikhi Ansiklopedisi (*The Encyclopedia of Islamic Jurisprudence)* Istanbul, Risale Basin-Yayin Ltd. 1990

INDEX